THE
MECHANIC MUSE

THE
MECHANIC MUSE

Hugh Kenner

New York   Oxford
OXFORD UNIVERSITY PRESS
1987

Oxford University Press

Oxford   New York   Toronto
Delhi   Bombay   Calcutta   Madras   Karachi
Petaling Jaya   Singapore   Hong Kong   Tokyo
Nairobi   Dar es Salaam   Cape Town
Melbourne   Auckland

and associated companies in
Beirut   Berlin   Ibadan   Nicosia

Copyright © 1987 by Oxford University Press, Inc.

Published by Oxford University Press, Inc.,
200 Madison Avenue, New York, New York 10016

Oxford is a registered trademark of Oxford University Press

Library of Congress Cataloging-in-Publication Data

Kenner, Hugh.
    The mechanic muse.

    Derived from talks commissioned for the 92nd St.
"Y," New York City.
    Includes index.
    Contents: In memoriam Etaoin Shrdlu—Eliot
observing—Pound typing—[etc.]
    1. English literature—20th century—History and
criticism.   2. American poetry—20th century—History
and criticism.   I. Title.
PR473.K38   1987   820′.9′00912   86–8482
ISBN 0-19—504142—9 (alk. paper)

2 4 6 8 9 7 5 3 1

Printed in the United States of America
on acid-free paper

In Memoriam Hugh Williams

Author's Note

For commissioning the talks from which this book is derived, I am grateful to Shelley Mason of the 92nd Street Y in New York City. A. Walton Litz suggested subsequent improvements, and in enhancing I've borrowed a paragraph or two from an article published in 1980 by *National Review*. The appendix, "Science, Axel, and Punning," is offered as a different perspective on instances the book surveys. It was prepared as a talk for a Syracuse University occasion in 1979 and first printed in *Syracuse Scholar*, II.1, 1981.

Contents

In Memoriam Etaoin Shrdlu   3

Eliot Observing   17

Pound Typing   37

Joyce Scrivening   61

Beckett Thinking   83

Epilogue   107

Appendix: Science, Axel, and Punning   113

Index   133

THE
MECHANIC MUSE

et ignotas animas dimittunt in artes

In Memoriam
Etaoin Shrdlu

1

You never see Etaoin Shrdlu in the newspaper now. Time was when you'd come across a whole line of print—

Rsoovelt etaoin etaoin shrdlu shrdlu shrd

—where you saw how the linotype operator had botched the start of the line ("Rsoovelt"). Then his shortest way to get the botch out of his machine's system was to fill out the line with nonsense, and cast it like any other line, intending to throw the cast slug away the instant it was cool enough to handle. But he'd get distracted and forget to throw it away, and if proofreaders got distracted too the line ended up in the paper.

His quickest way to obtain nonsense was to run his finger down either of the two leftmost columns of his keyboard, triggering ETAOIN or SHRDLU in that order. And why those letters in that order? Because they are the twelve most frequent letters in English, and a powerful reason, overriding human convenience, had placed them where they obliged the operator's left little finger to make an absurd 51 percent of his keystrokes. That reason was the machine's inherent complexity, which at all costs had to be kept within practicable bounds. The most frequent letters required the speediest handling.

For consider just some of what was going on. Every time the operator stroked a key, a little brass matrix ("mat") dropped out of a storage bin ("magazine") to ride down to its place in the line he was forming. Then molten lead forced against the assembled mats made a cast image ("slug") of the completed line. While the new slug cooled in a "galley" where slugs accumulated into newspaper columns or book pages, an arm swung down, snatched the used mats up, and sent them travelling back to their slots in the magazine. Amazingly, a linotype under decent maintenance almost never fumbled any of its hundreds of mats, and seldom squirted molten lead at a passerby. It was reliable because its countless linkages were all kept as direct as possible. The keyboard layout was an aspect of that. The letters ETAOIN SHRDLU were where they were just so the most numerous mats—the E's, the T's—could make the shortest journeys.

Today keyboard linkages are electric, via silicon patterns, with no reason not to put any key anywhere you like. So they use the familiar typewriter arrangement, and Etaoin Shrdlu has faded into history.*

Ottmar Mergenthaler patented his linotype in 1885, at the center of the decade when the instigators of High Modernism were born (Picasso, '81; Stravinsky, Joyce, Wyndham Lewis, '82; William Carlos Williams, '83; Pound and Lawrence, '85; Eliot, 88). That was also the year *Huckleberry Finn* was published, as if to remind us how Mark

---

* The corresponding typewriter "word," as every typist knows, is "Qwerty," and that arrangement had the express intention of slowing fast fingers so the early typebars wouldn't tangle. It persists because nobody wants to learn anything better.

Twain lost his shirt on a rival scheme to set type mechanically. For "reading matter"—so called, and what a name—was the chief mass-produced commodity of those years, and many were the entrepreneurs who foresaw fortunes in mechanizing a labor-intensive industry. Twain was shrewd in sensing that; he merely backed the wrong scheme. The one he backed was located in the Colt plant at Hartford, typesetting machinery being unthinkable save for the small-arms technology the Civil War had spurred into making thousands of durable identical parts. (Thus the first typewriter with a shift-key bore a rifle-maker's name, Remington.)

The linotype, manufactured by the thousand and at one time a multiple fixture in every newspaper plant in America and most printing houses that manufactured books, is as complicated a piece of lever-and-gear technology as you'd want to think about. Though, yes, reliable, it was so intricate it was very near unworkability; that was why many schemes, like the Twain one, failed. It is the fine flower of the golden age of ironware, when every thinkable human activity save perhaps the reproductive was being mapped onto machinery. The machine that fed Charlie Chaplin corn on the cob—the cob, like a typewriter carriage, zipped past his teeth and rotated—is a memorable 1936 takeoff, though by '36 the movement was obsolescing. The linotype had been especially bold in straddling two domains: of the foundry (hot lead) and of the fingers (mats, slugs), so combining founder's sweat with compositor's dexterity.

And, especially on its dexterous side, it illustrates two principles: (1) that the way to imitate a human activity is never to replicate the human action; (2) that the resulting pressures on human behavior are apt to elude fore-

7

sight utterly, and be occulted from most present sight, to leave hindsight flabbergasted. Who'd have thought we'd remember Mergenthaler for Etaoin Shrdlu? And a footnote to ".)eatondph 1/8 ador dorador douradora" [*Ulysses*, 16.1257]* should record that "eatondph" is the grope of James Joyce's memory toward "etaoin." He was trying for a plausible "line of bitched type" in a newspaper, and it's one of the few things he didn't get exactly right.

Who'd have thought, either, that the way to set type mechanically was something other than the time-honored way, picking letters up one by one and setting them in place? But that wasn't how to do it: matrices would slide down from magazines onto a moving belt for delivery to the line's incrementing array; and between the words wedge-shaped spacers would be pressed, which in squeezing everything out toward the boundaries would make all the spaces in any line identical. That bypassed all the skill with hairline spaces for which master compositors had earned respect. Likewise paper got folded—your newspaper was folded—not by applying steel fingers to sheets but by streaming a continuous fold between two rollers. When your copier jams it's because it has been forced back to the human state of fumbling with single sheets; your computer's printer thrives on a continuous perforated accordion-folded web. Continuity, stream, defines any machine's preferred fodder. You feed horses at intervals, but gasoline engines steadily. The fuel pump supplies an intravenous flow, such as humans get only when they're most remote from autonomy.

---

* Episode 16, line 1257, in the Hans Walter Gabler critical edition (1984). All previous editions preserve three errors the first printer made in transcribing this contrived error.

Etaoin Shrdlu affected the linotype operator somewhat, and the newspaper reader slightly, and yet it is an emblem. Its very obsolescence helps lend it status. It recalls, for one thing, a feature of those years, when human behavior, e.g. movements of one's left little finger, could be inflected by imperatives one needn't know about. (How many operators knew why ETAOIN had the leftmost keyboard column?) Technology tended to engulf people gradually, coercing behavior they were not aware of. And it altered their world, so much so that an office typist of 1910 could not have imagined how her 1880 counterpart used to spend the day.

In the twentieth century, said T. S. Eliot, the internal combustion engine altered people's perception of rhythm; little had been pervasively rhythmic earlier save one's own heart, one's lungs, the waves, and horses' hooves. X-rays (1895) made plausible transparent planes of matter (Picasso), the wireless superimposed the voices of twenty countries (*Finnegans Wake*), newsreel quick-cutting helped prompt *The Waste Land*. Words moved on wires; distant voices sounded in your ears; you could traverse London or Manhattan underground. Candlelight was abandoned to romance; you could read by an englobed glowworm. "John Eglinton looked in the tangled glowworm of his lamp"—that sentence from *Ulysses* [9.225] may be literature's first close look at an incandescent bulb. At an earlier place, the word "candescent" is used of the soul five lines after a mention of library "glowlamps" [2.72, 2.76]. It's notable, too, that both these lamps are in libraries, where the newest technology—air conditioner, computer—is apt to turn up early.

And the linotype is an emblem of something else: of

9

intricate intelligibility. Complicated though it is, it performs sequential functions, and performs them in such a way that by watching carefully for several minutes you can grasp what is going on. When that long arm swings down to collect the mats you can see how it gets hold of them, and how, having swung up, it feeds them to the turning shaft that will move them sideways till they arrive above their proper channels and drop. The contrast with, say, a transistor radio could not be more extreme. About that, your eye will tell you nothing; nor about the workings of a screen-and-keyboard terminal, with the aid of which most "type" is "set" today. (We will use the phrase, though real type is nearly obsolete.)

2

In that age of transparent technology, literature evolved parallel technologies of its own, "difficult," "obscure," before readers had formed habits of adequate patience, adequate attention. "Et ignotas animum dimittit in artes"— the motto to *A Portrait of the Artist as a Young Man* both claims the sponsorship of the fabulous technologist and warns us against expecting such a book as we've been used to. Arcane skills—"ignotas artes"—have gone into its fashioning, skills such as enabled the Wrights to triumph at Kitty Hawk. Their machine had nothing to hide—you could see every moving part—and yet it challenged comprehension, not least in never flapping its wings the natural way. They first flew it in December 1903; by 7 January 1904 James Joyce, twenty-one, had adopted the persona of Daedalus.

Next, *Ulysses:* a book as remote from old ways to tell a

story as the linotype is from the old way to handle type. Yet, intricately, its many stories get told: by no other means could so much life have been compressed between a single pair of covers. (Doing it the old way, Balzac had to envision 137 volumes, of which he lived to complete 91.) The day, moreover, that *Ulysses* reflects would have been impossible a generation earlier, before electric trams were moving people quickly about a large city. Dublin's tram system, in 1904 the world's most extensive, gets Stephen Dedalus from Dalkey to Sandymount, and Leopold Bloom from the baths to Sandymount, both by 11 a.m., Bloom again from Sandymount to Holles Street by 10 p.m., and but for those movings and the consequent sightings there'd have been no tale. Compared to progress on foot or even by hansom these shifts of location can seem instantaneous, an effect imitated by quick cuts between Joyce's episodes. ("Episodes"—city life was becoming episodic. A city shaped by rapid transit, and later by a telephone network, delivers its experience in discrete packets; the poet of *The Waste Land* was acutely sensitive to that.)

Like the technology of its time, Modernism sought to emulate human actions by means at once complicated and (by older standards) bizarre. A book like *Ulysses,* a poem like *The Cantos,* resembles in that respect one of those intricate feats of lever-and-wheel simulation.

There's a real connection, in short, between literary Modernism and what Richard Cork has called The Second Machine Age: the age, say 1880 to 1930, that saw machines come clanking out of remote drear places (Manchester, Birmingham) to storm the capitals and shape life there. The way the compositor's left little finger was commandeered by Etaoin, every city-dweller's sense of the

11

normal—precisely, of what needn't require attention—was gradually remolded by a thousand increments of technological pressure, from the cheap alarm clock to the dynamo. The tram-rides in *Ulysses* are so normal they don't even receive mention in the narrative, save for two entries, "Tramfare – 1d," in the record of Bloom's expenses.

A distinctive feature of High Modern writing is the kind of commentary it accumulates: the patient and incremental elucidation of details increasingly minute. Work on *Ulysses* has gone on for decades and is by no means done. The first business of commentary was to reduce gross obstacles to the book's being read at all. Then smaller units of difficulty were tackled. Finally, elucidation was disclosing unsuspected wonders, in effect removing difficulties we hadn't known we had. Post-finally, we ponder the status of the text, something that was taken for granted all along.

Bloom's budget for instance: the list of his day's expenses [17.1455–78]. For people accustomed to being told a story in the old way, the budget was but one more pedantic annoyance. What was such a thing doing in a novel at all? Justifying its presence meant supplying a rationale for the whole of the pedantic Ithaca episode, and once Stuart Gilbert had supplied that rationale (1930), the budget was something readers were willing to at least glance at. Its mere look on the page does convey much of its effect.

The second stage, inaugurated by Richard M. Kain (1947), entailed jobs like correlating the budget entries with the book's incidents. That disclosed Bloom's two tram journeys, elsewhere unrecorded.

It was two decades more before someone (myself, as it happened) noticed that the budget suppressed all record of the visit to Nighttown. Its most notable omission is the day's largest single disbursement (10s., left behind in the whorehouse.) So it's an *edited* budget, as it were for the eyes of Molly; that in turn relates the episode's question-and-answer format to the interrogation Bloom knows will attend his homecoming. Even in Ithaca, the episode of stony fact, fact is manipulable, including numerical fact: yes, number, the very atom of immutability.

And under the most recent scrutiny, the text itself commences to dissolve. For the budget went through several reworkings and at least two typings, in the course of which, seemingly by typist's error, the price of a square of Fry's chocolate shot up from £0–0–1 to 0–1–0. The balance Joyce then struck left £0–16–6 in Bloom's pocket, a sum compatible with the earlier statement [16.1697–8] that he had no coppers, having paid out the last of them in the cabmen's shelter. But the budget as printed in 1922 somehow restored penny chocolate, leaving the totals wrong. For a list of errata Joyce then recalculated, increasing Bloom's residual change to £0–17–5, and forgetting, as the Gabler edition points out [p. 1752], that five pennies do not comport with an absence of coppers. Gabler chose to preserve the consistency of *Ulysses* with itself by reverting to shilling chocolate. And that destroys another order of consistency Joyce valued, consistency with the real world of 1904, where I'm told that Fry's did sell for a penny.

The author, were he here, could put all this right by adjusting the sum he'd had Bloom start the day with. But the author is dead and the problem, within the limits of responsible editing, is now insoluble. Like physicists, Joyce critics can encounter a Heisenberg limit.

A corresponding narrative could be given of the critical

fortunes of most High Modernist works: *The Cantos,* for instance, or *The Waste Land.* First come efforts to justify the whole. Then units of attention commence to get smaller, and yet remain always discrete, like gears and shafts. The penultimate unit is the single word; the ultimate is the very letter.

> Between the two almond trees flowering,
> The veil held close to his side

—so a detail of Canto XX, as reprinted for years. But transpose two letters, undoing a compositor's error of 1930, and you gain both sense and sound:

> The viel held close to his side

—And lo, he stands, with his instrument, flanked by emblematic trees: himself an emblem in some manuscript illumination: and "viel held" sounds an emblematic chord. High Modernism's notations were spare; and, like a linotype's innards, though tough in function they were vulnerable to mishap. So much meaning has not often been at the mercy of a single misprint. That one lingered in the American edition forty years.

New ways of writing, then, for new orders of experience; urban experience; Modernism is distinctively urban. Like all writing it does modify earlier writing, partly because in continuity with the past lay the principles by which it could be understood at all. But like all live writing it ingests what's around it; as Shakespeare's was an age of fabulous voyages to the still-vext Bermoothes, Eliot's was a time of routine movement by tube—

14

Hampstead and Clerkenwell, Camden and Putney,
Highgate, Primrose and Ludgate.

How Eliot's verse derives from High Victorian verse is a
topic by now well canvassed; or what Joyce owed to
Homer and Sterne, Pound to Cavalcanti and even Bliss
Carman, Beckett to Synge and Yeats and Arnold Geulincx.
It seems time to sketch what they drew from the world
around them, not excluding the world-around-them's most
salient feature, intelligence questing after what can be
achieved by a patterned moving of elements in space: the
mats of a linotype, the words of a poem.

It's time also to remark how High Modernism did not
outlast transparent technology. Beckett, its last master, already carries it into the intangible realm of information
theory. And Beckett, it's become commonplace to say, is a
bridge to the so-called Post-Modern. That is: to our present world of enigmatic "text," of foregrounded codes and
redundancies, of microchips through which what moves
may be less interesting than the process of moving it elegantly. All of that absorbs, in Silicon Valley and at MIT,
intelligence of a rarified order. It's another subject.

Eliot Observing

1

Eliot has had an odd fate, akin to Milton's. He has not
been credited with noticing anything at all unless in a
book. It was a habit for decades to reconstruct his reading
lists, beginning with names he had himself supplied: Laforgue, Donne, Webster, Petronius. . . . These became
canonical lists, excluding as well as including, and their
look of maintaining fences seemed part of what the poems
meant. To read him was to claim admission to premises
where Shelley, say, was not mentioned.

A more recent fashion has been to map his emotional
idiosyncrasies, asking for instance how Charlotte Eliot's
youngest son, raised in a houseful of sisters, got to be so
aloof about women. We never ask what it's routine to ask
about Wordsworth or even Keats: what Thomas Eliot may
have observed when he opened his eyes, and what he made
of it.

Yet he called his first book *Prufrock and Other Observations,* and in its earliest poems, the first two *Preludes,*
an alert man in an American city is taking note of the new
century's novelties: for instance that the people of its cities
had submitted to being minutely governed by clockwork.
That was a new way to live:

> With the other masquerades
> That time resumes,
> One thinks of all the hands
> That are raising dingy shades
> In a thousand furnished rooms.

He wrote that about 1909, in Cambridge, Mass., and it now gets assented to, routinely, as an instance of urban sameness, urban routine. We seem not to ask how all those hands could have known, simultaneously, when it was time for the dingy shades to go up; the answer lies in the stamping mills of New England, where a small-arms technology the Civil War had perfected was mass-producing, for many thousand furnished rooms, the interchangeable wheels of a million cheap alarm clocks. Eliot, as so often, was bringing news. He had discerned, beyond the clocks, what the clocks enabled, the new world of the commuter, in which a principal event of the day was waking up in the morning under the obligation to get yourself somewhere else, and arrive there *on time*. And, unassisted by a public clock or a town crier, any number of people could now be imagined waking up at once. Measured in hours and minutes, not in days and lifetimes, Time was newly inexorable. Men measured out their lives with little ticks.

> Time for you and time for me,

as Eliot wrote elsewhere; time, as he wrote in the *Preludes,* to *raise* dingy shades, not open them. For the rooms are now equipped with pull-down blinds, their light-tight fabrics and their spring-loaded rollers two more small achievements of late-nineteenth-century technology. You need such appurtenances when your sleeping hours are no longer gauged by the sun.

Other rooms, less smartly equipped, still rely on wooden shutters. From the *Preludes* again:

> You tossed a blanket from the bed,
> You lay upon your back and waited;
> You dozed, and watched the night revealing
> The thousand sordid images
> Of which your soul was constituted;
> They flickered against the ceiling.
> And when all the world came back
> And the light crept up between the shutters,
> And you heard the sparrows in the gutters . . .

That, for Eliot, was the dawn of the twentieth century: a wakefulness brought by some clamor before the sun, to afford a little aimless introspection before it is time for your feet to join

> the muddy feet that press
> To early coffee-stands.

(Those coffee-stands are a boon if you've not had time for breakfast.)

It was the commuting that was novel. Being governed by time, it brought thousands into convergence, each person answering to a private time which yet was everyone else's. Mankind had never shared anything so abstract on such a scale before. When Christianity was shared it wasn't abstract. And the people whom commuting brought into one another's presence not only did not know one another, they did not even sense what it was they were all sharing.

> Each in his prison
> Thinking of the key, each confirms a prison.

21

Eliot by 1909 had been three years a student at Harvard, no stranger therefore to the world of the boardinghouse and the classes you attend on schedule. The conscientious student is governed by a timetable and by time.

> There will be time, there will be time . . .

Time to be questioned on the reading you are to have done—

> And time for all the works and days of hands
> That lift and drop a question on your plate . . .

Time for the library, time to rework the seminar paper—

> And time yet for a hundred indecisions,
> And for a hundred visions and revisions . . .

In *Prufrock* those phrases, of such evident undergraduate applicability, are subsumed into a ritual of social anxieties. True, classes at Harvard still had their social dimension, and professors still addressed their students as "gentlemen"—that was before the professor had become a tenure-track middle executive. Harvard professors even had students to tea. But it is not the obligation to go to tea that has turned J. Alfred Prufrock into a totem for millions of readers. It is the obligation to do only what others expect, to undergo their scrutiny without hope of escape, above all to turn up on time. That is the world of the modern office worker, to which Eliot's entree may have been the world of the undergraduate. In a world so defined, your only autonomous life is your interior life, and that is apt to be fragmentary.

2

Those poems are early instances of Eliot's extraordinary generalizing power. The world of the *Preludes* seems to be the world of office workers and factory workers, a world well outside the genteel young poet's experience. He felt his way into it from the experience he had, which was that of the student; also, from the experience of walking Boston streets, to observe

> the smoke that rises from the pipes
> Of lonely men in shirt-sleeves, leaning out of windows.

His own life was to be that of a pipesmoking lonely man; also the life of a commuter with some nine-to-five job or other, at Highgate School, at Lloyd's Bank, at the Faber office, in the furnished-flat world and the alarm-clock world. If his early poems join with his late ones, one reason is that the experiences they dwell on are continuous. The morning crowd in *The Waste Land* flows over London Bridge,

> so many,
> I had not thought death had undone so many,

crossing from the rooming houses south of the river to the banking and insurance offices in the city; and to St. Mary Woolnoth's striking of the hour

> With a dead sound on the final stroke of nine.

Here Lloyd's clerk supplied a candid footnote: "A phenomenon that I have often noticed."

The typist who comes home at teatime "clears her

breakfast," having left that morning in too much of a hurry to do the dishes. She then lays out "food in tins," and her dinner will entail no dishes. That is living in a hurry. She has knocked off work at the appointed hour, the hour

> when the eyes and back
Turn upward from the desk, when the human engine waits
Like a taxi throbbing waiting.

An elderly Eliot would be affluent enough for taxis, but even in his mid-forties he was commuting from South Kensington by underground: the Circle Line to Gloucester Road station, then the Piccadilly line to Russell Square, where the Faber offices used to be. To change from the one line to the other he had to "descend lower," as he puts it in *Burnt Norton*. One way down was by spiral stairs, on which you turned and turned the narrow gyre in half-darkness. That descent brought

> Internal darkness, deprivation
> And destitution of all property,
> Desiccation of the world of sense,
> Evacuation of the world of fancy,
> Inoperancy of the world of spirit;

—the subjection of body and senses to a featureless discipline of setting down foot after foot on iron step after iron step. But near the head of the stairs he could always choose a different route:

> This is the one way, and the other
> Is the same . . .

24

The "other" way was "the same" in two respects: it took
you down, and it numbed your sensibility. It was the electric lift, in which you and your fellow commuters did not
move, but the box you were all standing in did the moving; a descent

> not in movement
> But abstention from movement; while the world moves.

3

If Eliot is much else, he is undeniably his time's chief
poet of the alarm clock, the furnished flat, the ubiquitous
telephone, commuting crowds, the electric underground
railway. How his sensibility was shaped by such experiences grows vivid if we think of Yeats, whose address of
record was London from 1887 clear to 1918. Surrounded
by the advent of all these things, Yeats paid them no heed
whatsoever; it is a parodic effort just to imagine a Yeats
poem with a telephone in it. Yet in the years after 1900
Yeats was living through what Richard Cork has called
"The Second Industrial Revolution," which entailed nothing less than the mechanization of the whole city.

In their life of J. A. M. Whistler, a book Ezra Pound appears to have read to Yeats in the winter of 1913–14, the
Pennells, brother and sister, preserve a quaint detail about
1880's London: that its lanes were still scavenged by mu-
nicipal goats, turned loose at night. One frisky goat chased
a man whom Whistler knew right to the door of his club.
Those were the years too when Sherlock Holmes was hail-
ing hansoms, and they were years long gone by 1914, by
which time hundreds of mechanical taxis had been de-

ployed through most large western cities. Hastily commandeered, the famous "taxis of the Marne" in 1914 moved by internal combustion engine enough troops to save Paris. Yet in that year standing orders still required that on the third day of a general mobilization the swords of British officers should be sharpened, and railway cars that held forty men and eight horses—the infamous "quarante et huit"—remained normal behind the lines, though the horses no longer bore gallant men with swords but pulled big guns through mud.

You needed horses in Flanders Fields because muddy fields were trackless; that would not change till the invention of the tank. But inside big cities, by 1914 or so, the horses had virtually vanished, and in just about a decade. Needless to say, London's goats had vanished too. Cobblestoned streets had been hastily macadamed to accommodate the rubber-tired wheels; the huge drill which Jacob Epstein incorporated into a sculpture called "Rock Drill" was the sort of noisy thing you could see in the street outside your flat window, as the work of paving London and Paris went forward. Down beneath the streets ran the tubes of London, the metro of Paris: a mode of transport that had begun to be available at about the turn of the century, unthinkable before the locomotives were electrified. That in turn had been unsafe before the air brake, and impossible before the electric motor and the dynamo. Joyce in *Ulysses* records, as an arresting set piece, "the roar of flapping leather bands and hum of dynamos from the powerhouse" in mid-Dublin, 1904, serving the most advanced electric tram system in Europe; he also depicts the whole city frozen in paralysis when a dynamo quits. The big cities of Europe and northeastern North America were

26

turning into huge machines, primarily machines for shifting large numbers of people rapidly to and fro underground.

Buckminster Fuller reminds us how for generations it had taken Harvard students all day to visit Boston from Cambridge via Watertown Bridge. The subway that was opened in 1913 promptly cut a leisurely day to seven minutes. That had happened in Fuller's freshman year, and it led him, he says, to speculations about space-time acceleration and the finite velocity of light. His was one idiosyncratic response. T. S. Eliot's was different.

By the time they opened the Boston-Cambridge subway, Eliot was already a third-year graduate student. But, having spent a year in Paris, he had experienced one city dominated by electrified underground transport, and in London he would shortly encounter another, so possibly Cambridge had little more to teach him. He had already learned most of what he would use in his poems. One thing that seems to have impressed him was the capability of such systems for engendering crowds, such crowds as humankind had not routinely experienced before.

The members of a truly monstrous crowd cannot simply have walked into proximity. The day is too short. They need to be brought in rapidly in batches: moreover, brought somehow to the *center* of the crowd as it forms. Here the subway is uniquely enabled, since it can deliver new hundreds underneath existing thousands, for discharge upward into the thick of things.

The largest crowd I have ever myself experienced got estimated at 100,000, about the population of Duluth. It was assembled in a couple of hours and dispersed as rapidly. What made it possible was the electrified under-

J

27

ground transport of the city of Oslo. The occasion was an afternoon's ski-jumping, with 1,000 spectators for every participant. It seems a reasonable guess that a mob of similar magnitude gets pumped into central London every working morning, and every evening sucked out again. "Pumped" and "sucked" are appropriate metaphors; Eliot's most famous crowd *flows* across London bridge like a viscid liquid.

By nine, responsive to the morning clocks, the day's crowd will have been absorbed into the city's offices. Then, "under the brown fog of a winter noon," it will disperse through the streets toward the lunch counters; and a third time, "at the violet hour," its clerks and typists with weary eyes and backs will be sucked back underground for dispersal to furnished rooms, many of these equipped with what is sumptuously called, by salesmen, a "divan," and can also serve as a bed.

Later decades' dreary facts were novel once. Such a crowd-life, conducted in clock-bound synchrony, was in Eliot's young manhood a new order of human experience, accessible moreover only in the great capitals. That is one reason for Modernism, with its percussive rhythms (the rhythm of the internal combustion engine, as he once noted) and its rectilinear lines (the lines of subway plans and gridded streets), to have come exclusively from the great capitals, the capitals with subways, London and Paris; also why Modernism was the invention of people who had come to the capitals from remote places, to be struck with sudden comprehensive novelty. Its urban predecessor, the literature of Augustan Rome, was likewise the work of provincials. Vergil from marshy Mantua, Catullus from Sirmio, Ovid from the Abruzzi, Horace from Venusia, Juvenal perhaps from Aquinum, Sextus

Propertius from what they now call Assissi: such men, and not one of them born in Rome, have done for our idea of Rome what Tom Eliot from Missouri did for our idea of a London wholly changed since the time of Dickens and Conan Doyle.

New in crowded London, he did not fail to observe how in contrast with American crowds, where people look ahead, "each man fixed his eyes before his feet." London pedestrians do that still. If that struck me on my first visit there, it was thanks to air travel, which enabled an overnight comparison with New York. Eliot in the slow days of the steamer had had to rely on a more tenacious attentiveness to trivia. His small talk, as I experienced it on that visit, was apt to be of small things, on which, as for his master Sherlock Holmes, life and death if not indigestion might sometimes depend. He enjoined me to look *right*, not *left*, before stepping into a street. I had not been aware of my North American habit of looking left. But it was the sort of thing Eliot was aware of.

4

And now, to confront his eerie generalizing power, let us look at the *Waste Land* passage again with its separate observations fixed in place:

> Unreal City,
> Under the brown fog of a winter dawn,
> A crowd flowed over London Bridge, so many,
> I had not thought death had undone so many.
> Sighs, short and infrequent, were exhaled,
> And each man fixed his eyes before his feet.
> Flowed up the hill and down King William Street,
> To where Saint Mary Woolnoth kept the hours
> With a dead sound on the final stroke of nine.

There is that quotidian mass of London pedestrians, each one with eyes on the pavement. They sigh as they move up the hill; that they are sedentary beings, in no condition for uphill trudging, is one more trivial detail. Yet Eliot can make such observations sound as though rooted in a vision of Dante's and as portentous as anything in the *Commedia*.

"There I saw one I knew"—in such a crowd, a memorable event!—and immediately two Englishmen begin to talk of their gardens. That is a staple of English small talk, and in *The Waste Land* it sounds like this:

> That corpse you planted last year in your garden,
> Has it begun to sprout? Will it bloom this year?
> Or has the sudden frost disturbed its bed?

"That corpse"? Well, sure enough, we may think, Eliot is being literary again, and his literature runs to the King James Bible, where a seed dropped into the ground is compared to a corpse. Except it drop into the ground and die, it has no future.

But Eliot was more likely reading the daily papers, where the goings-on of murderers receive loving attention; and, once again, his transatlantic eye has been seized by a bizarre local commonplace. The English murderer declines to trust in distance; he prefers his corpses interred where he can keep an eye out. In New York they'll ship a pickled stiff to Los Angeles, or sink it in a concrete jacket in the East River. But Crippen put his victim under the cellar floor. Later in *The Waste Land* we shall hear of bones "cast in a little low dry garret," and in just a few years Sweeney Agonistes will be telling us of the man who did the girl in and just "kept her there in a bath / With a gallon of Lysol in a bath." So we needn't be surprised by nightmare garden-talk about

That corpse you planted last year in your garden.

Advice about gardens is a staple of talk like that, and we hear some, savagely jocular:

> O keep the Dog far hence, that's friend to men,
> Or with his nails he'll dig it up again!

—a doggerel rhyme, like the rhyme in "A stitch in time saves nine." A rhyme like that pertains less to "poetry" than to practical rules of thumb, which is what this couplet is; you'd best keep it in mind if you don't want dogs scratching up your prize roses, your prize corpses. It is hearty, friendly advice, spoken by one old messmate to another; for

> Stetson!
> You who were with me in the ships at Mylae!

is merely a grandiloquent transposition of what *Sweeney Agonistes* will be offering in the demotic:

> We were all in the war together
> Klip and me and the Cap and Sam . . .
> I'll tell the world we got the Hun on the run.

All that, based on the kind of sidewalk chitchat that would have been routine in London in 1920, takes Eliot's generalizing power toward the grotesque, a direction it often took. His method, as has often been noted, was to collect scraps of verse written at various times until he could see a way of fusing them; and the principle of fusion was apt to be that words cut loose from a specific context can assume strange scope and range. We've hinted that

> And time yet for a hundred indecisions,
> And for a hundred visions and revisions

are lines that might conceivably have been prompted by an overdue seminar paper. But, attached to Prufrock's strange surname, they come loose from whatever prompted them. And Prufrock's strange name, which Eliot noticed as a boy in St. Louis (though the responsibility for "J. Alfred" seems to have been his alone), sufficed to create a persona and a focus for a poem which might otherwise have been called, after Tennyson, "Supposed Confessions of a Second-rate Sensitive Mind."

There's a story of young Eliot walking home from dancing class with a girl who would one day be the mother of W. R. Burroughs, the eminent junkie. Mrs. Burroughs is reported to have told her son how they paused by the Prufrock-Littau Furniture show window. A bridal suite was on display, and the caption read,

> You Get the Girl.
> Prufrock Does the Rest.

Be that as it may, literally nothing of Prufrock survives in Eliot's poem except his name at the top of it, and the name is enough to draw the parts together. Drawing loose parts together was a title's function, and an Eliot poem tended to begin with loose parts. Thus we have it on Pound's authority that the "Prince Hamlet" passage—

> No! I am not Prince Hamlet, nor was meant to be;
> Am an attendent lord, one that will do
> To swell a progress, start a scene or two . . .

—was "a choice early bit" that Eliot didn't want to give up. Quite probably, like a number of bits that ended up in *The Waste Land,* he wrote it with no notion of what its eventual context would be. A mere title would later ensure that it was J. Alfred Prufrock, not Tom Eliot, who wasn't meant to be Prince Hamlet. We know too that *The Waste Land* found its title very late, something that may also have been true of *Prufrock.* And it is evident how much each title does toward establishing the poem we know. Transmuted by a title's focus, all the observations written down at various times lose sight of their first bearings. Eliot was not teasing when he protested more than once that his intention was irrelevant to our experience. One thing he meant was that lines he could have conceived amid struggles with a late term paper have lost touch with anything specific. Another thing he said more than once was that he had "quite forgotten" what he once meant; this means, probably, that he'd lost track of some long-ago first context, which surely portended less than the final poem.

So it's routine for things he observed to be unrecognizable, even to him, once embedded in a poem. That needn't stop us from speculating on what may once have been their literal sense. So it's likely that a detail from *Ash-Wednesday,*

> The lady is withdrawn
> In a white gown . . .

simply records the way Vivien Eliot looked when she was hospitalized with her wretched nervous disorder. But the full quotation runs,

The lady is withdrawn
In a white gown, to contemplation, in a white gown.

And how the word "contemplation" masks that clinical possibility! Some years ago, too, a BBC documentary on Eliot raised the possibility that *The Waste Land*'s "falling towers" and "hooded hordes swarming / Over endless plains / Stumbling in cracked earth" may have been literal impressions of World War I newsreels.

5

Speculation is free; his unique way to make poems permits it. So let's venture one more suspicion, that in addition to crowds and commuters and alarm clocks, Eliot's poetry responds to yet another of the new century's pervasive experiences, that of being talked to by people we cannot see. This happens whenever we pick up a telephone, a thing we do so many times a day we quite overlook the strangeness of what happens next. A character in *The Cocktail Party* remarks that you can't tell the truth on the telephone, meaning probably that you lose three quarters of your communicative power when you cannot be seen and your breathing body is absent, and you must fabricate mere semantic sequences. Your words are only a fraction of what you say, and the telephone throws you back on nothing but words. It is in *Sweeney Agonistes,* the play that gives the telephone bell a wholly metrical speaking part, that we hear the famous phrase, "I gotta use words when I talk to you."

When the phone rings in that play—

Ting a ling ling
Ting a ling ling

34

Dusty snatches it up and says,

Hello Hello are you there?

—which is what they used to say in England (in 1956 I heard it there myself at least twice), and is also, as the accurate Eliot would have observed, a question to which the answer ought to be "No." No, I am not "there," even though a voice like my voice is in your ear. When I talk to you on the telephone, what is present to you is my phantom presence, a voice not even in the room where you are, the way a ghost's voice would be, but exactly in your head. Eliot belonged to the first generation of poets to have such an experience. And he seems to have been the only poet who took notice. His training in phenomenology may have been his resource.

It is very notable in Eliot's poetry, and especially in *The Waste Land*, his first major work after he'd taken up residence in London, how the numerous voices of the poem have no locality and observe no occasion; how the poet himself seems disembodied, unlocatable; how very much the speeches rely on words, how little on context. Among the first telephones in literature is the one we hear Leopold Bloom using in *Ulysses:* an instrument in a business office on which he is trying to reach a man named Keyes, at his place of business, on a matter of business. That scene is dated 1904, when the phone was still what Alexander Graham Bell had in mind, a facilitator of business, like the cash register. Apart from the toys of a few wealthy folk, a telephone where people merely lived was unthinkable. Bell himself thought it unthinkable, and would not have one in his house. A mere twenty years later, by the date of *Sweeney Agonistes*, we are unsurprised to find a phone in Doris's walk-up London flat. In so brief a time the city had been wired. And people had acquired the habit of attending to disembodied voices, and returning them routine answers. It is as queer as any transaction with a ghost in Shakespeare.

But no one (save perhaps Tom Eliot) thinks it queer; because imperceptibly, amid distraction from the false analogy of the telegraph, everyone's sense of how voice relates to person has been altering profoundly. *Words*, those seem primary, and neutral; a *voice* is no more than a means of making them audible, and it may as well issue from an earpiece as from a face. So we're apt to take Sweeney's "I gotta use words" as an instance of lowbrow Sweeney's inarticulateness, forgetting the hyperarticulate Prufrock's "It is impossible to say just what I mean": impossible, to be sure, when the needful gamut of gestures is socially interdicted, and your collar mounts firmly to your chin and holds your head upright. You might as well be talking on the telephone.

So *The Waste Land* is, so to speak, a telephone poem, its multiple voices referrable to a massive short-circuit at the central exchange. Ezra Pound had no telephone, no radio. Yet the century co-opted him the moment he reached for a different machine. We'll encounter him typing.

Pound Typing

1

In August 1925, in his fortieth year, Ezra Pound, in Italy, seated as usual before a machine, was sending off to America for photographs of machinery. His father, Assistant Assayer at the Mint in Philadelphia, responded with a photo of the Medal Press in the Royal Mint of England. Ezra called the picture "magnificent," and instantly wondered, "Why can't the Uncle Sam mint do something as good in the way of photos of its internal workings." A good question: it was like the questions he'd long been asking about the poetry in the *Atlantic*. As every visitor to Philadelphia knows, what the Uncle Sam Mint has for sale is celebrations of its exterior encasement, much as what magazines had on display was the look of the sonnet. Soon Ezra Pound was reflecting that a government headed successively by Wilson, Harding, and Coolidge wouldn't know that the Mint had any insides.

He has not been alone in remarking American incuriosity about machines and processes. A quarter-century later Sigfried Giedion, the Swiss historian of technology, would express amazement that the Ford Motor Company had no records of the mass-production techniques it had pioneered, no photos or working drawings of its assembly-line machines. Rather than preserve these, Henry Ford had elected to restore Greenfield Village, a kind of museum of procedural archaisms. By contrast, the Kensington Science Museum, a short walk from where Ezra Pound had lived in London, shows you automata that spun and pounded inside Victorian factories. British antiquarian sentiment finds these as interesting as Ezra found the Royal Mint's coin press.

The English photo was just the kind of thing he was looking for. "The NOSE of the big dies, for example, excellent shape. Photos of the detail of the coin press, especially at the point where force is concentrated. NOT the damn detail of the *coin,* sentimental symbolism. Miss Murphy the Belle of the Bowery. Liberty before she was lost."

For it was perfectly clear that the face on the coin was some random American face that had caught some depictor's attention. Artists pick faces at whim; the Pre-Raphaelites had picked shop-girls. Long before, in Greece, a coin could offer the profile of a goddess. But by 1915, when the U.S. Mercury dime and Liberty half-dollar got designed, artists were willing to let their eyes get caught by "Miss Murphy" next door. Calling her "Liberty" didn't make her transcend mortality; nor did the artist's skills rival Pisanello's. So by 1925, Ezra Pound was finding the coin press more interesting than the coin. It contained, he said, "the point where force is concentrated." And that point was no longer to be found at the tip of the engraver's chisel.

2

It is to be found in the innards of a machine; machines had once been an era's impassioned expression. Like all expression they manifested grades of excellence; at their best, unredundant, austerely impersonal, they concentrated on their work with an iron Nijinsky's precision. In London, historic capital of the Machine Age, Wyndham Lewis had written of a "disastrous polished dance," and suggested that engineer and artist might well become transposable terms. What was congenial about machines was their perfect absence of self-consciousness. They never showed off; every move was purposeful. That quality had recently caught the attention of Pound's Paris friend George Antheil, whose *Ballet mécanique* seemed a score for robotic choreography.

This fascinating and profoundly serious work was meant to be *performed* by a machine: a player piano for which Antheil prepared the rolls, punching notation for percussive rhythms inhumanly exact, and for chords no human fingers could execute. The *Ballet mécanique* in that medium is nearly unknown; the piano rolls somehow disappeared for decades, to emerge from a closet in Los Angeles only when Antheil was long dead and Ezra Pound near death. Instead a concert version has achieved mild notoriety, its orchestra augmented by airplane propellors and foghorns: a publicist's stunt, a romanticizing of mere clamor. That order of facility was always Antheil's weakness. He enjoyed notice as "The Bad Boy of Music." Yet in scoring his composition for mechanical piano he'd managed to pose a truly radical question, whether connoisseurs of music did not themselves romanticize the varnished viols and shiny brasses of obsolete salons.

The purposeful ballet he'd celebrated was performed openly; you could watch the parts at work. Oddly, at about the time Antheil's piano rolls disappeared, the encasement of machines was coming into vogue. The thirties' catch-

41

word was "streamlining," advertised as a formula for enhancing efficiency and actually a program for concealing
the evidence. That was a far-reaching aesthetic decision, as
essentially Victorian as the mythical trousers on table legs.
I can remember seeing a streamlined milk-wagon; the
horse who was pulling it may not have known that the
aerodynamic drag on his load had been minimized.

But before that, when the coin press was a visual guide
to its own workings, the mind of the machine could be
observed in its focus on a point of exquisite concentration.
Into that space a new blank is slid; next the nose strikes
down with a force that embosses the blank on both sides.
Then the nose is withdrawn, while a new blank replaces
the new coin. In the vicinity of that point of impact everything happens. So, Pound, 23 October 1925,

> The good forms are in the parts of the machine where
> the energy is concentrated. Practically NO machines show
> high grade formal composition; the minute they hitch
> different functions, or . . . have parts NOT included in
> the concentration of the power, they get ugly, thoughtless.

"Parts not included in the concentration of the power":
that rhymes with the second clause of the 1914 Imagist
Manifesto: No Unnecessary Word. And note the phrasing,
"They get ugly, thoughtless": beauty is attention, beauty
is incarnate thought. Ugliness, the absence of beauty, is
not perversity but lack of thought. It is when a poet isn't
thinking, when he's filling out for instance the rhyme
scheme of a sonnet, that his work grows empty, ugly. That
is also what happens when a designer is specifying the
parts his machine needs just to hold it together. Pound
might have adduced the sewing machines of that era,

adorned with irrelevant gilt curlicues everywhere save where something serious is happening: where the needle plunges through a presser-foot slot down a hole exactly aligned, to transact its momentary business with the bobbin beneath. It was when the Singer designers weren't concentrating on that crucial transaction that they relapsed into ornament. Ezra Pound, analogously, had cut *The Waste Land* by removing the lines in which Eliot could be seen filling out a scheme. Those were also the lines in which energy was not being concentrated.

> . . . Bestows one final patronizing kiss,
> And gropes his way, finding the stair unlit;
> And at the corner, where the stable is,
> Delays only to urinate, and spit.

The last two lines were there because a quatrain required them. Twice elsewhere on that page the word "perhaps" confirmed that Eliot did not always pretend to know what was going on. Where energy was not being concentrated, Pound's blue pencil slashed. That had happened in December 1921, and it's continuous in principle with the 1925 letters about machines.

And those letters reaffirm the Vorticist affirmation of 1914:

> The vortex is the point of maximum energy.
> It represents, in mechanics, the greatest efficiency.
> We use the words "greatest efficiency" in the precise sense—as they would be used in a text book of MECHANICS. . . .
> Every conception, every emotion presents itself to the vivid consciousness in some primary form.

It is the picture that means a hundred poems, the music that means a hundred pictures, the most highly energized statement, the statement that has not yet SPENT itself in expression. . . .

Hugh Selwyn Mauberley's "urge to convey the relation / Of eye-lid and cheek-bone / By verbal manifestation" was an urge ill-directed. He should have been drawing pictures, but in the wrong medium he fussed his energies away.

3

Energy, efficiency, concentration; and two other criteria of Pound's were "accuracy" and "impersonality." A tool-and-die maker could underwrite that aesthetic. And not the least of the nineteenth century's artists were its artisans, men possessed by a new passion for nonredundancy. A suspension bridge by Isambard K. Brunel can command more sustained respect than *The Idylls of the King*. So can a poem such as Pound's 1912 *The Return*.

The first thing we need to do with such a poem is *see* it on the page: its irregular stanzas, its regular left-hand margin, its equally regular secondary margin that runs exactly down the middle. The first stanza, three long lines and a short, looks like a stanza of Sappho's: not as Sappho wrote it, but the way nineteenth-century editors had learned to lay out her words on a printed page, to help our eyes grasp the symmetries of a lost tune. But as we scan down Pound's page we watch Sappho's stanza disintegrate; what is returning now is "uncertain" and "wavering" and "slow" and "pallid." And this judgment has the force of a community, no single voice but a choral presence, the words coming from the left hand and from the right, united in deploring a wraith-like deficiency of vigor.

THE RETURN

See, they return; ah, see the tentative
Movements, and the slow feet,
The trouble in the pace and the uncertain
Wavering!

See they return, one, and by one,   5
With fear, as half-awakened;
As if the snow should hesitate
And murmur in the wind,
                    and half turn back;
These were the "Wing'd-with-Awe,"   10
            Inviolable,

Gods of the wingèd shoe!
With them the silver hounds,
            sniffing the trace of air!

Haie! Haie!   15
        These were the swift to harry;
These were keen-scented;
These were the souls of blood.

Slow on the leash,
                    pallid the leash-men!   20

The next thing to notice is the clean efficiency by which
the poem is structured with one simple device, the present
tense versus the past:

        See they return, one, and by one,
        With fear, as half-awakened;

but

        These were keen-scented;
        These were the souls of blood.

45

And finally, listen to

> The trouble in the pace and the uncertain
> Wavering,

—the metrical insecurity that accompanies the present-tense lines; and to

> Gods of the wingèd shoe!
> With them the silver hounds,
>   sniffing the trace of air!

—the strong beat, dactyl, spondee, catalectic spondee,

$$x ^{\wedge \wedge} \mid x \, x \mid x$$

that speaks from the old time when the unembodied had "souls of blood," to be contrasted now with theology's impalpable wraiths or nostalgia's thin fantasies.

They were the "keen-scented," the "swift to harry": they were concentrations of imaginative energy, not to be mimicked by plaster casts in classrooms, nor yet by the facile Pre-Raphaelite rhythms of that generation's fashionable translator of Greek tragedies, Professor Gilbert Murray (who, Eliot was to say, "erected between Euripides and ourselves a barrier more impenetrable than the Greek language").

The Return assembles myriad details, visual, acoustic, semantic: such details as the off-rhyme,

> Haie! Haie!
> These were the swift to harry,

as though the English verb "harry" were a mutation of a cry, "haie!," that might have been Greek. The details, though, are not fitted into a framework, like the framework of a sonnet, to hold them in place; they are simply present to one another in the same way as the stars that make up one constellation. Here it's helpful to adduce a distinction from one of Pound's 1925 letters about machines:

> . . . MUST distinguish between machinery, motor parts, and mere static structure. The static structure in machines really part of architecture and employs no extra principle. Governed purely by form and taste.
>
> It's the mobile parts, and the parts REQUIRED to keep 'em in their orbits or loci that I am interested in.

"Taste" is passive; "governed by taste" means governed by habit, like the Singer giltwork, which was much of it Burne-Jones hand-me-down like the endpapers of the old Everyman's Library.

To attend to this poem is to pay heed to an intricate process, all in plain view. It has no mysterious designs upon us, no formal concealments comparable to a streamlined shell, and we are entitled to see everything that is at work. That is one reason what we see looks a little diagrammatic. And Pound's ideal poem would consist solely of "mobile parts" and "parts REQUIRED to keep 'em in their orbits or loci." The parts required may include, as we have seen, the placing of the words on a printed page. That entailed exchanges of notation, unavailable to Sappho, among (1) a recipient who could be expected to *see* the poem, not merely, like Sappho's audience, hear it sung; (2) a scribe (as we now say, a printer) who can reproduce visual instructions exactly; and (3) a way of creating the poem in one's workroom in a form close to the form in which it will be printed. So *The Return* is an early example of what has become a twentieth-century genre, a poem that could only have been composed on the typewriter.

4

So we come back again to the machine, and it grows important to ward off misunderstanding. The Industrial Revolution is notorious for having decentered many million lives, and from the Blake of the "dark satanic mills" to the Yeats who linked "mechanical" with "servile"—

> And never stoop to a mechanical
> Or servile shape, at others' beck and call

—in short, for a span of a century and a half, the word "machine" has accordingly been made to connote somnambulism, ennui, misery and idiot repetition.

But somnambulism and idiot repetition were exactly what Pound's generation thought it could see machines putting an end to. As Buckminster Fuller, just ten years Pound's junior, wrote in 1940,

> The inherent
> the **social** meaning of **Industrialization**
> . . . seems least of all understood
> by the professional
> painters, architects, novelists, and clergy,
> who have seen the price
> that men have paid for it,
> without understanding what they were paying for. . . .

Much work entails much repetition, and a machine should be doing that, to augment a man's leisure. Imagine the

labor of inscribing *The Return* by hand, letter aligned
with letter the way printing will reproduce it. But a typewriter lets you do it in two minutes. Likewise, as we read
toward the end of the eighteenth Canto,

> And the first thing Dave lit on when he got there
> Was a buzz-saw,
> And he put it through an ebony log: whhsssh, t ttt,
> Two days' work in three minutes.

"Two days' work" on an ebony log would entail many
thousand fatiguing mindless strokes with a muscled arm,
and it's difficult to argue that a man condemned to such
toil is well off. Or a man condemned to set pages into type,
letter by letter by hand. The linotype abridges four hours'
toil to one. Not that the setting of fine books by hand
need be obsolete: in 1925, the very year of the machine-
letters, William Bird at his Three Mountains Press set *A
Draft of XVI Cantos* in that way. A man like Bird, though,
could take time over such a fine folio precisely because
the bulk of book production had been mechanized for a
generation. Artists could even buy handpresses cheaply
because job-printers had discarded them.

Before there could be buzz-saws, metallurgists had de-
vised alloyed steel for the blade, and machines to cut teeth
around the rim of a steel disk had been imagined and constructed too, and also ways to sharpen each of these teeth,
and shafts and bearings and lubricants and tractable
sources of power. Technology arises from, and creates,
interdependent communities that do esoteric things well;
you put trust in colleagues you need never have met. Here
Fuller is eloquent:

> However,
> man unconcernedly sorting mail on an express train

with unuttered faith that
the engineer is competent,
that the switchmen are not asleeep,
that the track walkers are doing their job,
that the technologists
who designed the train and the rails
knew their stuff,
that thousands of others
whom he may never know by face or name
are collecting tariffs,
paying for repairs,
and so handling assets
that he will be paid a week from today
and again the week after that,
and that all the time
his family is safe and in well being
without his personal protection
constitutes a whole new era of evolution—
the first really "new"
since the beginning of the spoken word.

That's down-to-earth. Pound by contrast tried to imagine the origins and continuities Fuller was content to abridge with the word "evolution." His characteristic historical vision disclosed glimpses of a continuous imaginative current running through the entire story of mankind, manifested now in one form of activity, now in another. Sometimes he offers this under the figure of an underground religion, its tradition coursing for instance

from the San Ku

to the room in Poitiers where one can stand
casting no shadow

that is Sagetrieb,
　　　that is tradition.

Builders had kept the proportion,
　　　did Jacques de Molay
　　　　　know these proportions?
and was Erigena ours?
　　　Moon's barge over milk-blue water
Kuthera *deina*
　　Kuthera sempiterna
　　　　　　Ubi amor, ibi oculus.
　　　　　　　[Canto XC]

The San Ku, in China, ten centuries B.C., was a three-man council charged by the emperor with making the world's germinative energies shine forth. The room in Poitiers, some 2500 years later, is the microcosm of a world suffused by light. Erigena said that all things that are are lights. And Kuthera *deina,* Kuthera sempiterna, the terrible and eternal goddess of beauty, proclaims her motto, "Where there is love there is sight."

Pound wove many such chains of continuity; and according to one of them, the nineteenth century—a low time for sculpture (the Albert Memorial), for painting (Watts's "Hope," which looks despairing) and for poetry (even Swinburne a stuck needle)—had husbanded like all times its legacy of imaginative energy, but not where the aesthetes were looking; no, in machine shops and in the tool and die works and among the minds that conceived the rotary press, the typewriter, the linotype, the sewing machine. He delighted to quote a tailor named Blodgett who had thought sewing machines would never come into general use. *There* spoke the perennial art critic. It was

51

Blodgett's intellectual descendants who'd hooted at the Post-Impressionists.

The imagination that had flowed into such contrivances was like the kind that had manifested itself in the verses of Sappho, prizing the swift and the sure and always clear about its aims, and certain of where the energy was to be concentrated. It was preserved in blueprints and metal the way Sappho's had been fitfully preserved on parchment. It economized human toil the way art like Sappho's economized and concentrated human perception, human expression. Leonardo, who painted pictures and wrote sonnets and also designed machines, may have been the last man to understand in his bones how these three activities are unified at their root, and he was hampered by a technology which could not realize his machines. Thus he designed a clumsy bicycle that would have needed wagon wheels, for lack of the high-tension steel that might have let him conceive wire spokes.

For history keeps turning on simple inventions. The scale on which things could be done after the Middle Ages depended on the invention of the horse collar, which enabled teamed horses to move such weights as Egypt had assigned to human shoulders by the hundred. Draft horses in their horse collars enabled craftsmen to erect St. Peter's. Later, to adorn the site, a 361-ton obelisk was ferried from Egypt, and a few dozen horses pulling turnstiles round and round tensed the cables that hauled it upright in one day. And it is very striking that when Ezra Pound offers his outline of the story of literature, he assigns the key role to a small group he calls "The Inventors." Like high-tension steel, a rhythm can be an invention. So can a stanza like Spenser's. The sonnet, serviceable for a couple of centuries, had been an anonymous invention. Pound himself had invented, when he used the shifting margins of *The Return* to indicate that more voices are speaking than one. One effect of a poetic invention is to diminish the number of words.

Poems are made of words, but of more than words. They are made of all the devices by which the words, and the way we hear them or see them, can imply melody, and gesture, and intonation, even facial expression. So a Sextus Propertius who speaks English is made to say,

> And it was morning, and Cynthia was alone in her bed
> I was stupefied
> I had never seen her looking so beautiful
> No, not when she was tunicked in purple
>
> Such aspect was presented to me, me recently
> emerged from my visions;
> You will observe that pure form has its value.

Two inventions in particular are drawn on here. We see one when the line "I was stupefied" floats between "Cynthia was alone in her bed" and "I had never seen her looking so beautiful," to let us register a double take. The other is the exploiting of unstated contexts; thus "pure form" is a formula in which art critics seek refuge when they must discourse of nudes, and "aspect" is a British euphemism for the human posterior. We gather that Cynthia is not only alone but unclothed, and that her visitor thinks it best not to specify this. It is all done in fifty-one words, a crystal of faceted economy.

Though its author is Ezra Pound, its presiding "inventor" is perhaps Henry James, whose oeuvre Pound had just finished reading entire, prior to surveying it for the James memorial issue of *The Little Review*. A highly formal utterance about "pure form" would have been James's way to cope with a naked lady, had he found himself under such a necessity. He once summarized the cheering at a Harvard football game as illustrative of "the American capacity for momentary gregarious emphasis." Such a manner is an indisputable comic invention, no more a pathology of James's personality than the light bulb is a pathology of Edison's. That you did not have to be James to use James's discoveries was something Pound proved by using them in a poem James wouldn't have understood. And as most of us switch on the light without thinking of Edison, so thousands have read the *Homage to Sextus Propertius* without entertaining a thought of the polysyllabic Master. Many have supposed that its idiosyncrasies came straight from the Latin.

5

So Pound, born 1885, was born late into the century of the machine, of large coordinated enterprises designed to concentrate energy, reduce effort, and annul duplication. Once we persuade ourselves that "machine" need not connote iron nor hardware, that the word applies to any economical self-activating system for organizing resources, we can see mechanisms everywhere in the century, most impressive in the century's resourcefulness at organizing and making accessible all that could be ascertained about the record of human speech.

That was the ruling passion of three generations of learning. Its epic poem was the *Oxford English Dictionary*, which coordinates the work of many thousand toilers to the end that users can get light on intricate questions by consulting a single entry. Railways and the penny post helped make it possible, and machines to cut note-takers' paper into uniform sizes, easy to alphabetize. Systems of sorting and filing had been worked out over the decades, in part by postal clerks. Uniform printed books with numbered pages made accurate citation feasible. The steel pen, which obsolesced the quill and the penknife, had doubled the words a clerk could scribble per hour. Entailing volunteer readers by the hundred, filling out printed forms to precise specifications, the enterprise soon resembled a coordinated meta-machine, its subordinate parts arrayed the length and breadth of Britain, its point of concentration the office where the finished entries were distilled. The entry on the verb "set" alone was a decade or more in the compiling and extends to two-thirds the length of *Paradise Lost*. And the great work was served by a thousand ancillary works, all of them exquisite concentrations of intellectual energy. They included the annotated and footnoted editions of as many of the writers of the world as expertise could get hold of. Ezra Pound was an undergraduate when the great editions were still coming out, and his debt to them was lifelong. Their lore irradiates his poetry.

Thus in a recent essay Fred Robinson has helped us watch Pound's negotiations with the Anglo-Saxon *Seafarer*, as he pursues single words through the labyrinth of Clark Hall's *Concise Anglo-Saxon Dictionary* and weighs alternatives offered by the notes to Sweet's *Anglo-Saxon Reader*. Collectively, notes like Sweet's resemble a machine in bringing many hours' investigation by many peo-

ple to one place where a glance can suffice. For the sole
and settled meaning some scholars like us to think they
possess is sheer illusion. Old poems—*The Seafarer* is very
old—exist only as approximately accurate markings on
paper, which until we have learned a great deal have no
meaning whatever.

Sometimes, even to a learned eye, the markings make
no sense at all, and scholars must guess. They guess with
the aid of what other scholars have made of similar markings elsewhere. And as for dictionaries—how anyone knows
with confidence the meaning of a single Anglo-Saxon word
is a subject it would take an hour to begin to elucidate.
Dictionary entries are apt to be lists of options, and the
"right" interpretation is a chimera.

There was a time when scholars toiled in isolate darkness, aiding one another by happenstance correspondence.
But by 1912, when Ezra Pound made his *Seafarer,* Hall's
Dictionary and Sweet's *Reader* had made thousands of
hours of work by dozens of men accessible at a glance. The
place where the energy is concentrated is in the fine print
of the apparatus, and it is fascinating to watch Pound lin-
gering there. Robinson has rendered forever untenable
the old image of a half-educated guesser at a language he
didn't know. (Pound's college yearbook described him as
"Bib's pride," and "Bib" Ibbotson had been his Anglo-
Saxon teacher.)

Thus from *wuniath tha wacran* he got "Waneth the
watch," not by substituting for the ancient words modern
words that look rather like them, but by drawing on a
note from which he learned of scribes elsewhere confusing
wuniath, survive, with *waniath,* wane, and on a dictionary
from which he learned that *wacran,* though it generally

meant "weak," could also be a form of a word meaning "watchful." If you think that *wuniath* is correct as written and that *wacran* means "weak," you get "The weak survive." If you follow Pound's trail you get "the watchful ones wane," hence his "waneth the watch." If you follow his process, even though you may reject his decision you learn what it is to care about the meaning of words, which is important learning, more important than any single guess about syllables a thousand years old. "Waneth the watch" has been jeered at by accredited scholars. Such a scholar is someone who knows a non-scholar is wrong, and need not say how he knows it. His union card suffices.

But there is a scholar of another stripe, whose concern is to help you to what he knows. It is his work that's epitomized in those book-machines, the nineteenth century scholarly editions. And nothing is more striking, as we look over Ezra Pound's long career, than his habitual reliance on people who knew what he didn't know, and made their knowledge available. The roll call is extensive: for Anglo-Saxon Sweet and Hall; for Provençal Canello, Levy, Lavaud, a dozen more; for Chinese Fenollosa, Legge, Morrison, Mathews, Karlgren; as for Italian, one of his published essays details for thirty pages his dealings with expert opinion on just one poem of Cavalcanti's. Of his indebtedness for Latin and Greek, suffice it to say that some of the odder things in his *Women of Trachis* derive from nineteenth-century footnotes of Jebb's.

Concentration of energy, that was what he found in their books; a willingness to save someone else the time they had themselves expended. Likewise the designer of a machine saves you time; the typewriter alone saved Ezra Pound countless hours. All you have in this life is time, and whoever helps you save it confers a boon. A poem too is time-conscious; "an intellectual and emotional complex in an instant of time," was the way Pound described poetry's primary pigment, the image. It strikes you with the pleasure of great intensity, moreover speedily. And rhythm, which governs the poem, is "form cut into time." For time is a span allotted.

> wave falls and the hand falls
> Thou shalt not always walk in the sun
> or see weed sprout over cornice
> Thy work in set space of years, not over an hundred.
> [Canto XLII]

The wave, the hand, these fall; but every age has its way to imagine what can outlast mortality, and the generations whose imagination Pound inherited could conceive of a fine machine, its parts whirling in purposeful ballet, according to the three-dimensional choreography of a very high order of human intelligence. More attention, we've seen, went into designing the coin press than into the design of the 1916 U.S. dime, a sculptor's impression of some girl next door ("Miss Murphy").

As it happens, we can particularize. The name of the sculptor in question was Adolph Weinman, and the girl next door, in New York in 1915, was named not Murphy but Elsie Kachel Stevens. Her face is on the half-dollar and the dime, and one day her husband, a burly lawyer named Wallace Stevens, would be able to stride through his club in Hartford, Connecticut, jingling a pocketful of his wife's effigies. That will not have been something Pound knew, and Wallace Stevens's place in American poetry is not part of our narrative. That the story brushes past Stevens at all is pure fortuity, the sort of thing Aristotle cautioned us not to build plots on. A story to irradiate the mind is built of what is necessarily so, and for a good metaphor of necessity we may look to the interaction between the descending die in the press, and the shuttle that feeds in new blanks and expels finished coins, implacable as Greek fate. And it's another story entirely, though not unrelated, that Pound came to see the fate of all civilization concentrated in the issue of coinage.

Joyce Scrivening

1

Cities entered the twentieth century by different routes, and at different paces. Dublin got there thanks to some entrepreneurs from Cork, who came up to a seaport city with the worst slums in Europe, one of the world's most notorious red-light quarters, and an infant mortality rate surpassed only by Calcutta's, and managed through their genius with creative finance to equip it with the most advanced electric tram system anywhere. In the process, of course, electric power stations got built, and the habit of maintaining the lines got established. Dublin is still a city where getting a telephone can take two years, but the power department's emergency crew will tumble into overalls at 2 a.m. at word of an outage.

If your trouble is in a buried line they will rip up the pavement and dig. Once they've left, though, they leave behind a hole, perhaps big enough to swallow several pedestrians, and the filling-up of that hole may not happen for weeks. Routinely, a crew will be sent to watch the hole. They will pitch a tent over it and settle in for a long stay, equipping the tent with necessities of life: a primus stove, a teakettle, a cribbage board. It takes three men to watch a good-sized hole. Day after day they will watch it, and no one will steal it, until the day when, mysteriously, a lorryful of men with shovels arrives; soon after which, lo, the hole is filled and gone.

Such bursts of active and then contemplative power mark the Dublin rhythm. People are either in a great hurry or in no hurry at all, and are sometimes expending their maximum of energy while in the latter state. A good Irish storyteller could derive a whole entertainment from the goings-on in the tent, over the cribbage board, all the weeks when nothing is happening to the hole. The *Irish Times* once ran a feature called "The Hole"; week by week, it simply recorded the chat of men watching holes. The most flourishing local industry is the manufacture of sentences, and somehow everything, even electrical technology, always gets brought into the service of that.

Time is suspended in a dream of intricate talk. In the pawn shop where I once tried to purchase some coins, there could be no business done until the shopkeeper and his crony had canvassed thoroughly the prospects of yet a third duffer who was coming forth, it seemed, from an old folks' home to seek his fortune in the labor market. "And what will he be doing? Is it falling off of buses? Why, he's older than the Chinese."

On the whole, the phrase "labour market" is an anomaly. You are Halloran the pawnbroker or Sweeney the dentist, as though enrolled lifelong in a craft guild. Joyce devoted ten lines of *Ulysses* [15.1427–36] to a phantom procession of "coopers, bird fanciers, millwrights, newspaper canvassers, law scriveners, masseurs, vintners, trussmakers, chimney sweeps, lard refiners . . ." and so on up to thirty-three different callings, like the turnout for a feast day in the Middle Ages. Dublin has even, as he did not fail to notice, a "Sick and Indigent Roomkeepers' Society" which apparently looks after you if you are a dues-paying roomkeeper fallen sick or indigent. Its name is still emblazoned on its office windows. Anyone who is a room-keeper presumably knows what the word means. Like much English encountered in Ireland, "roomkeeper" is not in the O.E.D.

A reason may be that the O.E.D. relied on printed sources, and by the time idiosyncratic Irish usages were getting into print a good deal of the dictionary's data had already been gathered. In 1910 P. W. Joyce, no kin to James, published *English as We Speak it In Ireland,* so frequently reprinted it testifies to a market for what was perceived as Irish quaintness. Irish quaintness is what stands out against a background of "standard English," and standard English is English like the wallpaper, the English you don't notice. Thus in the 1890's nobody noticed when an English poet was using the ubiquitous iambic pentameter, and W. B. Yeats could create a sensation by starting from an iambic line with *six* stresses and inserting one extra syllable just before the caesura, to get something that was neither iambic nor pentameter. An iambic pentameter line might have run,

> I will arise and go to Innisfree.

But Yeats did not write that, nor did he write

> I will arise and go, and go to Innisfree,

which would have exhibited the six-stress iambic rhythm of his friend Ernest Dowson's

> Last night, ah, yesternight, betwixt her lips and mine.

No, Yeats's line runs,

> I will arise and go now, and go to Innisfree,

with a wavering result that fell on enchanted ears as "Celtic." His fan mail for that one poem included a letter from Robert Louis Stevenson in Samoa.

But there was a way to satisfy the market for Irish quaintness that did not require the talent of a Yeats, and that was the normal method of Victorian prose fiction, which had worked out elaborate codes for exhibiting what always preoccupies a British reader, the social class of the characters. The principle is easily stated. You commence with a "neutral," literate idiom, called the narrator's. That is the idiom the writer shares with the reader. In itself it is not noticeable at all, but other idioms become visible by deviating from it. Deviations of diction and syntax are common, also deviations of rhythm. Any of these signals the presence of a "character," and repeating the pattern makes the character recognizable. To indicate oddities of pronunciation you deviate systematically from standard spelling: an elementary instance is the Cockney's dropped aitch.

The novelist, in short, can create "characters" out of tricks with diction and spelling. In James Joyce's boyhood, that was how Irish speech lived, when it did, on printed pages. Thus in 1899 Edith Somerville and her cousin "Martin Ross" published the first of their immensely successful *Irish R.M.* volumes. The narrator is English, and so is the narrative idiom: perfectly featureless because its purpose is to be the blank screen against which "Celtic" deviations are projected, in passages like this:

66

'Why then 'tis here he lives indeed, in this little house, and a poor place he have to live in. Sure, he's my son, the crayture————' her voice at once ascended to the key of lamentation—'faith, he didn't rise till today. Since Christmas Eve I didn't quinch light in the house with him stretched in the bed always, and not a bit passed his lips night or day, only one suppeen of whisky in its purity. Ye'd think the tongue would light out of his mouth with the heat, and ye'd see the blaze of darkness in his face! I hadn't as much life in me this morning as that I could wash my face!'

We note "crayture" and "quinch" and "ye" to mark odd habits with vowels; one exotic word, "suppeen," to mark an idiom essentially foreign; also other tricks unnecessary to list. And we know that we are dealing with someone not as privileged as we: both "Irish" and imperfectly educated. "Her voice at once ascended to the key of lamentation"—that is the narrator's language (and ours) and the character in the story would be incapable of it.

2

Now here is James Joyce, in the first lines of a novel:

Once upon a time and a very good time it was there was a moocow coming down along the road and this moocow that was coming down along the road met a nicens little boy named Baby Tuckoo. . . .

His father told him that story: his father looked at him through a glass: he had a hairy face.

He was Baby Tuckoo. The moocow came down the road where Betty Byrne lived. She sold lemon platt.

> *O, the wild rose blossoms*
> *On the little green place.*

He sang that song. That was his song.

> *O, the green wothe botheth.*

When you wet the bed first it is warm then it gets cold. His mother put on the oilsheet. That had the queer smell. . . .

The first thing odd about this page is the look of it: little paragraphs mixed with italics, and not a quotation mark in sight. The "neutral" narrative idiom has disappeared: the literate and hardly noticeable idiom that forms the usual common ground of reader and writer. It was from this common ground that the narrator would extend a helping hand, explaining what the odd behavior of the characters meant, and illustrating it with quotations. But if the narrative idiom has disappeared, then for practical purposes the narrator has disappeared too, and we must fend for ourselves amid textual indications which include, in the very first sentence, three words we have never seen before: "moocow" and "nicens" and "Tuckoo." Next we must translate "glass" into "monocle," a word Baby Tuckoo wouldn't have known; and "had a hairy face" we interpret as "bearded."

If the narrator has disappeared, where is the text coming from? It is certainly not coming from a baby; the words are correctly spelled and the sentences accurately punctuated. Moreover it is in the third person: "He was Baby Tuckoo." Let's agree to say that it's present on a printed page, thanks to the intricate and largely anonymous mechanisms by which that can be made to happen. We look at printed pages all day long without ever reflecting on how so many thousand letters got there. The Victorian novelists got into the way of exploiting printed pages, but do not seem to have quite reflected that that was what they were doing. Though they freely employed the convention of misspelled words to indicate dialect or want of education, they seldom worked free from the implicit presence of a storyteller. It is well known that Dickens wrote to be read aloud, preferably by himself: the death of Little Nell came most alive when Dickens was reading the chapter to an audience. Misspelled words once served like details of musical notation, to cue a storyteller's change of voice. And James Joyce's most radical, for that matter his most un-Irish act, was dispensing with the storyteller. He forces us to confront printed pages, and make what we can of them.

Outside of fiction, this was nothing new. Reflect that the *New York Times* does not tell you stories; it simply exhibits column after column of print. The headlines, where many readers glean most of their information, are invariably anonymous, and the idiom they speak is Headlinese, meaning nobody's. Beneath them we find the details, in smaller print. Some of the columns of detail are "by" so-and-so, some are not. But the presence of a byline doesn't matter to you and me. It is not as though the owner of the byline were *telling* us. The *Times* is telling us. The one place bylines matter is inside the *Times* organization, where they attest the status of reporters who have a future. The *Times* does keep in its employ a few resident personalities, whose bylines do matter to readers, but these are not entrusted with news; a Russell Baker or a Tom Wicker gets confined to a special page, there to amuse us or to have opinions. Achieving that status is the ultimate dream. But it cuts its holder off from what the

69

newspaper claims to exist for, the impersonal processing of daily news.

The newspaper's massive anonymity had been achieved by the time James Joyce had learned to read. It followed from the implications of the printed page, where words look just the same no matter who wrote them, and their location in space—front page vs. inside pages—is what assigns them status. These implications had been noticed by Mallarmé in France but by no one, so far as I know, in the English-speaking world: certainly not by English fiction-writers, who still used the page as a mass-reproducible substitute for the storyteller's speaking voice. Joyce alone seems to have understood from the first what it can mean to be writing for print. Each stroke of his pen encoded instructions for a print-shop technician, a fact of which he was at all times fully aware.

His first published fiction appeared in a trade paper, amid ads for milk pumps and cream separators, and it represented Irish speech in this fashion:

—Mind you, I noticed there was something queer coming over him latterly. Whenever I'd bring in his soup to him I'd find him with his breviary fallen to the floor, lying back in the chair and his mouth open.

She laid a finger against her nose and frowned; then she continued:

—But still and all he kept on saying that before the summer was over he'd go out for a drive one fine day just to see the old house again where we were all born down in Irishtown and take me and Nannie with him. If we could only get one of them new-fangled carriages that makes no noise that Father O'Rourke told him about—them with the rheumatic wheels—for the day cheap, he said, at Johnny Rush's over the way there and drive out the three of us together of a Sunday evening. He had his mind set on that. . . . Poor James!

When she gets one word wrong—"rheumatic" for "pneumatic"—she does so without hesitation; she's not being funny. And there's no comic spelling here. That is because the narrative does not presuppose a "normal" pronunciation by which to gauge hers. Nor is there anything in the way of "quaint" idiom for outsiders to quote: she is not being put on exhibit to amuse outsiders. And her utterances are minimally punctuated: a comma here and there to mark a slight pause. Otherwise the long undulant strings escape being Steinese by virtue of internal rhythm, a rhythm to which the transcription is scrupulously faithful, though it's up to us to reconstitute it. "Whenever I'd bring in his soup to him there I'd find him with his breviary fallen to the floor, lying back in the chair and his mouth open." There are many ways to put that into grammatical English:

Whenever I'd bring his soup in to him there . . .

Whenever I'd bring him his soup in there . . .

Whenever I'd bring his soup to him in there . . .

We may be sure that our author has tested them all and found the only one with the right speaking cadence: "Whenever I'd bring in his soup to him there." As for "lying back in the chair and his mouth open," that "and" denotes an idiom of the Irish language, exerting pressure on Anglo-Irish usage. It is accurate and conveys no special quaintness.

71

The issue of comic misspelling deserves attention. Prior to *Finnegans Wake* Joyce reserves it for just two situations: when a speaker is drawing attention to his own pronunciation, because imitating some foreigner, English ("Wy don't you old back that owlin mob?") or Yankee ("Wall, tarnation strike me!"); and when nature, not culture, interferes with speech, as when someone has bitten off the end of his tongue: "—I' 'ery 'uch o'liged to you, sir, said the injured man." Otherwise the murkiest Dublin dialects receive the same orthographic courtesies accorded to university men. We detect their presence by syntax and cadence alone.

Note: *we* detect. We become Joyce readers the way we become newspaper readers: by practice. In neither case is there a narrator to help us. We are simply engaging the technology of print, and starting to be qualified once we are free to forget that it is a technology: once the page has ceased to *look* odd. At our earliest stages of engagement with Joyce, we stare at his page and wonder how to get a purchase on it. Most browsers still get no further with *Finnegans Wake;* at one time, to be staring at the page was the normal condition of gapers at *Ulysses;* and one of the earliest readers of *A Portrait of the Artist as a Young Man,* Edward Garnett, publisher's reader for Heineman's, reported that the last part of what now passes for a fairly tame text looked utterly fragmented.

3

No writer was ever so observant of the way our lives have come to be governed by marks on paper. The characters in *Ulysses* are reading and writing constantly; those acts occur in virtually every episode. At one point Leopold Bloom receives a typewritten letter from a woman he has never met; one of its sentences runs, "So now you know what I will do to you, you naughty boy, if you do not wrote." [5.252–3] Bloom notices this—"Wonder did she wrote it herself"—and Joyce means us to notice it too, and to reflect not that Martha is illiterate but that "i" and "o" are adjacent keys on a typewriter. Elsewhere [16.1260] Bloom's name appears in a newspaper list of those present at a funeral, but misprinted: "L. Boom." I once struggled to quote that in the teeth of a publisher's editor who kept trying to correct my "error." I was fortunate in winning that round. Joyce himself did not always win. The 1968 Penguin edition of *Ulysses,* the one sold throughout the world except in the U.S. (and in '71 "reprinted with corrections") has Martha typing ". . . if you do not write," and Bloom pointlessly asking, "wonder did she write it herself." That records the interference of a British proofreader as long ago as 1932. It remained for Hans Walter Gabler's critical edition of 1984 to restore "wrote" in both places.

Of Gabler's 5,000-odd corrections, the vast majority entail, as here, a single character only. It is difficult to dismiss any as unimportant, so closely is Joyce's work bound to print-shop technology. Whether by hand or by keyboard, printers set single characters, one by one. Correspondingly, Joyce's unit of attention is apt to be the single character. If you saw "did she wrote it herself" in *David Copperfield* you'd assume a printer's error. When you see it in *Ulysses* you are correct in asking what it may mean. Assuming an uncorrupted chain of transmission, it will surely mean something. "Boom" means that an imaginary typesetter was dozing. "Rere" distinguishes the Dublin term for "back" from "rear," pronounced "rare," what parents do with children. "Eeleven" [5.94] catches a speaker's deliberative shift of stress. In "It ruined many a man the same horses" [5.825] the absent comma after "man" notes a Dublin rhythm (unhappily blurred when Gabler by a rare misjudgment preserves a typist's comma). Some fifty exclamation marks in the first episode were meant to show Buck Mulligan exclaiming like a hearty fellow in 1900's fiction, though all but half a dozen of them got lost when a typist who hadn't known how to fabricate "!"—apostrophe, backspace, period—got tired of emending by hand. (Gabler gives us back all those important "!"s.)

Joyce meant to assert final control over every mark on the final printed page, clear down to the dot with which Ithaca terminates ("Comme réponse un point bien visible," he instructed the printer). Arranging, rearranging—he once told Frank Budgen that he had the words but was seeking their appropriate ordering in the sentence—he seems guided by the analogy of compositors' fingers arraying cubes of metal. And the surprising amount of *Ulysses* that was actually written on the margins of proof-sheets—for instance, 34 percent of the Ithaca episode—prompts the reflection that the sight of the printer's artifact, its text extricated at last from his own execrable handwriting and his typists' irregular transcriptions, tended to prompt his most expansive flights.

So it is unsurprising that so much of his biography can be reduced to a string of imbroglios with printers. When he wanted something "wrong" they'd put it "right." When with infinite pains he'd arrived at nonstandard rightness, then they'd tend to make it wrong. (An officious foreman's pen altered Bloom's panic-stricken "Ah soap there I yes"

[8.1192] to "Ah, soap there! Yes.") And sometimes when he wanted something perfectly innocuous they'd balk absolutely. For print, as he discovered early in his life, is the most arcane of twentieth century mysteries. We have even a category of words we call "unprintable."

Such a word was "bloody," and an English publisher for his first prose book, *Dubliners,* backed out because no printer would set that word in type. After the book was finally printed in Ireland, by a publisher whom the bloodys in Synge's *Playboy* had not stopped, the sheets got destroyed uncirculated having after all trespassed the limits of printability. This time the offending words included the names ·of several Dublin pubs: Davy Byrne's, the Scotch House, Mulligan's. The Irish publisher panicked. He may have objected to giving those three houses free advertisement. More likely, he feared lawsuits, notwithstanding that Joyce had caused nothing unseemly to go on, unless you count boastful talk as unseemly, and had even offered to get explicit permission from the pubs in question.

We're reminded how Victorian convention would assign fictional happenings to the year 18—, in the city of B———, and may marvel that Joyce was bold enough to name his city, Dublin, and in *Ulysses* to assign a year, a month, a day, and even to specify actual street addresses. Leopold Bloom lives at 7 Eccles Street, and Paddy Dignam's funeral procession starts at 9 Newbridge Avenue, Sandymount. Those are actual houses (both vacant in 1904, according to Thoms' Directory), and the prospect of setting in type what is actually *so* can affect printers like a religious taboo. It is like uttering one of the names of God.

That extreme of boldness was reserved for *Ulysses;* on the surface, *Dubliners* seems vague by comparison. Still, anyone familiar with the city can frequently identify actual buildings; recall that the publisher who destroyed the sheets of *Dubliners* was a Dubliner who knew the place well. But *Ulysses* names actualities wholesale, even to William Miller, plumber, with toilet bowls ("bare clean close-stools") in his window at 17 Duke Street [8.1045]. We commence to understand why *Ulysses* had to be typeset in Dijon and published from Paris.

Had Joyce's been boldness for boldness's sake it would have been perverse indeed, seeing the misery it caused him. But as early as *Dubliners,* when he stood by his costly decision to name those pubs though it meant his book going unpublished two more years, he was guarding what could not be surrendered, the deep congruity on which his whole art turned, the congruity between the modern city and the printed book. Both are finding-systems; as a man sleeps at Eccles Street, no. 7, back room, so his name appears on page 5, line 3, fourth word. Both are subject to tacit zoning; as the district of Rathmines (Late Victorian shabby-genteel) is not the district of Rathgar (dingily arriviste), so the third episode of *Ulysses* (solipsistic, exotic) is not the seventeenth (objective, catechetic); in either case, experienced denizens suddenly arrived know where they are in an instant. Both employ undeformable units: bricks, typographic elements. An element misplaced is spotted at once by the skilled but can trap the unwary: the loose cellarflap Bloom circumvents [4.77] is like the typing error we're meant to notice. And both city and book are haunted by the shades of people: Dublin by many thousands in no real sense at home there, *Ulysses* by a vast roster of people whose voices, even, we may think we hear though it's we ourselves who silently supply them.

And in Joyce's fictions, the absence of a stable narrating voice makes one more parallel operative: we are set down in book as in city, virtual strangers, amid people who seem to know what is going on though we somehow can't ask them, and we learn to find our way and feel somehow at home, to the point where we may even notice things the natives don't seem to. From the very first Joyce let his readers sense that there was much going on they didn't quite understand. *Dubliners* is but a few hundred words old when we first hear someone speaking. This is Old Cotter, and we don't know what he's saying because he won't complete his sentences. "—No, I wouldn't say he was exactly . . . but there was something queer . . . there was something uncanny about him. I'll tell you my opinion." But he never does. The narrative goes on: "Tiresome old fool! When we knew him first he used to be rather interesting, talking of faints and worms, but I soon grew tired of him and his endless stories about the distillery." "Faints and worms?" That's never explained, though it sounds somehow morbid. One day we may learn from a big dictionary that both are distillery terms. But we shall never learn something after all more mysterious, what "endless stories about the distillery" could possibly be like.

Joyce delights in leaving us such queer things we may misinterpret, as if to keep alive in us an awareness traditional fiction is at pains to lull, the awareness that we *are* interpreting. The phrase "black mass" occurs in his story "Eveline," though as part of a clause about "the black mass of the boat." It's safe to feel sure he planted it, just as it's safe to state that when Macaulay, describing the trial of Warren Hastings, wrote the strange sentence "On the third day Burke rose," he was wholly unaware of alluding to a miracle. That is the sort of thing Joyce is *never* unaware of. When we find the word "grace" in the story called "Grace," it's embedded in the following sentences:

> Mr Kernan was a commercial traveller of the old school which believed in the dignity of its calling. He had never been seen in the city without a silk hat of some decency and a pair of gaiters. By grace of these two articles of clothing, he said, a man could always pass muster.

If we're inclined to think of "grace" as a word from the vocabulary of religion, well, so are at least five other words in that passage: "believed," "calling," "decency," "gaiters," and "articles." Here are they all, still keeping company with "grace," though souls are no longer at stake, only an archaic respectability. That, in fact, is what the story, "Grace," has to say about Dublin religion, that it has become the servant of respectability. If you're properly religious you're unlikely to fall down a pub's lavatory stairs and bite your tongue.

This clustering of vocabularies into overlapping fields is something Joyce took great pains with. It comports with the fact that all printed words, unlike words on living tongues, are absolutely neutral. We can't tell what they mean till we can size up their neighbors. (Structural linguists like to contrive examples. What does the word "flies" mean? The word "like"? It depends. "Time flies like an arrow," but "Fruit flies like a banana.")

4

Though print is always and everywhere potentially ambiguous, fiction dominated by a narrator contrives to minimize ambiguity to the point of concealment. Joyce, as his work progressed, was at pains to maximize ambiguity, to throw back on us all the implications of the fact that the signs we decipher can be maddeningly mute. His last work, *Finnegans Wake,* has a title in which "Finnegans"—as printed, no apostrophe—can only be a plural noun, hence "Wake" a verb, probably indicative. But whoever hears that title also hears the name of a nineteenth century comic song in which "Wake" is a noun and "Finnegan's" a possessive singular. The book commences with a word ("riverrun") that is in no dictionary, and it ends with the English definite article followed by nothing, not even by a mark of punctuation; and what's to be done about that, and about all the 200,000-odd words in between, is our responsibility solely. It's like being dropped down in a city where they're speaking all the languages of mankind simultaneously, and the one language we are fairly sure of is English. Like most travellers, we either give up or eventually make do.

It's basically English: even the distribution of its commonest words reflects English frequencies. Yet, as never before, the single letters control. "Laid to rust" says "laid to rest" and a little more. "Phall" says "fall" with extra torque. "Retaled" says "told again," but in being placed three words from "wallstrait" it receives fiscal contagion ("retailed"). These examples are from the book's first forty-one lines.

Amid so steady a bombardment it grows hard to lay hands on what you know perfectly well. "Common nown from the asphalt to the concrete"—Professor E. E. Stoll heard "abstract" and "concrete" but puzzled at "common nown"—"Come on down?" A professor of English, that is, couldn't hear "common noun." For he didn't *hear* "nown," he *saw* it, and it looked like "down." It would have been the "w" that caught his eye, forfending "noun," where the letter you notice is the "u."

The root phenomenon *Finnegans Wake* exploits is the utter silence of print. We look at it: that is our only course. Since we're literate, it sounds itself, silently. If it's irregular ("nown") we can make ourselves sound it—with an effort. But many of us are more likely to see something like "now down." "With half a glance of Irish frisky," was Joyce's example in a letter: "the words the reader will see, but not the ones he will hear." Seeing, hearing: the Gutenberg dissociation. "The Divine Comic, Denti Alligator" works because "Alligator" *looks* like "Alighieri," whereupon "Denti" creates serried teeth and locks two malapropisms into congruousness.

From the first words of *Dubliners*—"There was no hope for him this time; it was the third stroke"—where "stroke," in saying "cerebral accident," is not disentangled from strokes of inexorable clocktime, to the last words of *Finnegans Wake*—"A way a lone a last a loved a long the," where in shifting from noun to adjective, from definite article to indefinite, the sentence (sentence?) does not lose the spaces that permit us to count its words (11—Joyce's number of recommencement), James Joyce was aware always of silent print, and of readers now seeing, now sounding, always interpreting. It's odd, in the very last moments of Molly Bloom's monologue, to see "with the old windows of the posadas 2 glancing eyes a lattice hid," where "2" jerks us back from the phonetic realm so violently Joyce himself was surprised—he wrote "two" and then changed it—while pre-Gabler printers dropped the number altogether. "Two glancing eyes a lattice hid," runs the song Molly's remembering: music, incurably acoustic, though the look of "2" seems to say not. Penelope weaving and unweaving her web wove it, warp and woof, of sound and sight.

5

But back to the men whose job was to watch the hole. That is not a reasonable job. Holes do not get stolen, not even in a land where golfers are passionate. You may think the three men were there to keep pedestrians from falling into the hole. But their tent pitched over the hole should have obviated that; moreover while they were inside the tent playing cribbage they could not so much as see a pedestrian. There they played, on the city payroll, for several weeks. Their example can be commended to anyone who thinks events in Joyce pointless or unmotivated: who wonders, for instance, about a man who spends his entire day walking the streets but passing lampposts on the outside. That man is named Cashel Boyle O'Connor Fitzmaurice Tisdall Farrell, and his presence in *Ulysses* is utterly unexplained. He strides by from time to time, one time to mutter a Latin phrase, *Coactus volui,* which went unexplicated for sixty-three years.* Then there's a man named Gumley, whose paid job is to watch paving stones by night, and see (somebody remarks) "that they don't run away." Cities support all manner of seemingly pointless behavior. In finding odd ways for people to be gainfully employed, Dublin City is perhaps especially accommodat-

* In the Fall 1985 *James Joyce Quarterly* R. J. Schork traced it to Justinian's *Digest* and supplied a plausible reason for Farrell to utter it.

ing. Just recently I spotted there a red-bearded man whose daylong occupation was polishing parking meters. No one seemed to know if he was on the city payroll or not. No one is more oddly employed, come to think of it, than the James Joyce expert, of whom one or two make a living in Dublin, but many more all over the world. Their job, it may seem, is to watch the paving stones that they don't run away, or the holes that they don't get stolen.

They fill, though, it's widely agreed, a necessary office, difficult to specify. No other body of fiction so resembles a city in necessitating such guides and such watchmen. Nor does any other body of fiction so resemble a city in containing such holes into which the naive may fall, or such loose stones over which they may stumble. Like Dublin, it's shabby and intricate; like Dublin, it won't go away. Like Dublin, it exudes an ambiguous hospitality. Like Dublin, and unlike New York, it's much the same when you go back to it. There are guidebooks, and guided tours, and the way of the natives can seem both charming and bizarre. Joyce once said there was no higher human destiny than to be the mayor of a great city. He himself, though did fulfill a higher one, issuing instructions to typesetters in three countries, that they might erect according to his plans, each of them doing something as simple as laying bricks, constructions intricate as any city, made of letters on lines, and haunted, and solely for the enticement of visitors.

Beckett Thinking

1

Sam Beckett graduated from Jonathan Swift's College, Trinity of Dublin, where the library had contained a Sextus Empiricus for Swift to scan. From Sextus Empiricus Swift seems to have picked up the notion that Ulysses at the close of his adventures was metamorphosed into a horse. That is one reason for Gulliver, a modern Ulysses, to spend his last days in the stables talking to horses, apparently in their own tongue. As for what Beckett in his turn picked up from Empiricus, we may deduce it from Hamm's climactic speech in *Endgame:*

> . . . Moment upon moment, pattering down, like the millet grains of
> (*he hesitates*)
> . . . that old Greek, and all life long you wait for that to mount up to a life.

This theme was first stated, by Clov, in the first speech of the play:

> Finished, it's finished, nearly finished, it must be nearly finished.
> (*Pause.*)

Grain upon grain, one by one, and one day, suddenly, there's a heap, a little heap, the impossible heap.

Why is the heap "impossible"? Because it's derived from the favorite strategy of a man who delighted in proving to all comers that they knew not a thing, not so much as the meaning of the first word they might utter. More than once, he was ready with the "fallacy of the 'Heap.' " His Loeb editor enlightens us:

> Does one grain make a heap? Or, if not, 2, 3, . . . x grains? . . .
>
> *Outlines of Pyrrhonism, II, 253, note*

—"A heap, a little heap, the impossible heap." "Heap," as Mr. Spock used to say, "does not compute."

Sextus Empiricus, who flourished circa A.D. 190 (it gets put that way, though his tone seems not that of a flourisher) was a physician whose three volumes of *Pyrrhonean Sketches* tended to reduce all knowledge to ashes. For centuries he seemed an amusing spoilsport. But the signs that Swift read him in the 1680's go with other ominous signs, notably the popularity in those years of languages designed on the drawing board, never spoken by human lips, never stammered by babes, and thus inert to the skeptical acids. Such languages will contain no terms to which meaning cannot be assigned, since the terms will be produced not by the carelessness that makes do with words like "heap," but at the inflexible behest of the meanings themselves. Their designers start with a taxonomy of all that can possibly be meant.

In 1668, for example, John Wilkins D.D., Dean of Ripon and Fellow of the Royal Society, published his *Es-*

say Towards a Real Character And a Philosophical Language, a big book meant to order the unbridled impulses of Man the Naming Animal. Man in that role had been active ever since God charged Adam with naming the creatures, and was to persist into our century, into the CalTech Jet Propulsion Labs even, where mere red rocks seen in photographs from Mars got dubbed The Midas Muffler and The Dutch Shoe. For men cannot bear, it seems, to confront something and not name it, and this habit, never having been guided by method, has sown unspeakable confusion. A Dutch Shoe, on Mars? And what, they may be asking a thousand years from now, can "Midas Muffler" have meant?

"The Midas Muffler" would not have suited Dean Wilkins, who'd have whirled through the Jet Propulsion Labs like a white tornado. It is not for man, he'd have asserted, to assign labels at whim. No, man's job is to discern the operative categories first, and assign names afterward, keeping always a clear eye on the categories. Method will find us a right name for that rock. We might for instance take a survey of the Martian plain, and then name it by location, as X356—Y224.

In Wilkins's usage, you do not *call* a thing by its name, which would be arbitrary. No, you *use* the name to designate the thing's location in a taxonomic chart. The chart lays out the entire scheme of the world, and it branches and rebranches like a great tree. Thus the genus *Element* is called "De"; its Fifth Difference, a brightness in the air, is "t"; and the First Species of this Difference we designate by *"a",* pronounced like the *o* in *cot.* The first species of the fifth difference of genus Element is a rainbow, so we call a rainbow De + t + a, "Deta." That word marks a place in a system, the place where "rainbow" is located. The system, not the look of the rainbow, is our guide, and within the system Det*a* is the rainbow's real name, disentangled both from rain (for you can see it when you're not being rained on), and from any kinship with bows (which are something else entirely, the so-called rainbow being useless as a weapon).

In the age of Beckett, Wilkins's book is entrancing, so alike are its processes of thought to those of a Beckett character, a Molloy, a Malone. It launches into one of its most bizarre flights when the author must consider how adequate is his taxonomy of the beasts. For who knew what Creation might hold in reserve? Might beasts beyond counting, brought back from unknown lands, soon overburden his scheme? But this is the kind of question skeptics ask about the capacity of Noah's Ark, which is known to have carried members of all the species above the flooded world for a whole year. God, Who knew the tally of the creatures He'd created, had also dictated the Ark's dimensions, in cubits. The opportunity thus presents itself to refute in the same few pages both scoffers at Scripture and doubters of the System.

But first, the cubit. Earlier, both Origen and "St. Austin" (Augustine) had worried about the Ark's sufficiency, and had had recourse to an *Aegyptian Geometrical cubit* of 9 feet, familiar to Moses, the scribe of Genesis, from his time in Egypt. That does provide for a much bigger Ark. But it clashes with Goliath's stature as reported in the book of Samuel, making him 54 feet tall, and his head consequently "about nine foot in the height or diameter of it, which must needs be too heavy for *David* to carry." So we shall see instead what can be done with the common cubit.

Now God knew too, and must have pointed out to Noah, that the creatures would need food. In addition to the sheep carried to preserve the ovine species, sheep would be needed to sustain the carnivores; also grain, for the herbivores, and fruits or roots for the likes of the Sloth, the Squirrel, the Porcupine, the Armadillo. Each of the three kinds needed a common measure, to facilitate calculation. Let the unit of carnivore appetite be the Wolf; then two Lions will eat as much as four Wolves, two Tigers as much as three; the 40 individual carnivores (two each of 20 species) sum to the equivalent of 27 Wolves: say 30. Now since one Sheep is known to suffice for six Wolves per day, all Noah's beasts will require five Sheep daily, 1825 for the year, and it is easy to show (with the aid of a foldout diagram) that the Ark can carry them all, on its bottom deck.

In like manner Wilkins calculates the hay to be allowed for 26 kinds of herbivores, not forgetting those 1825 extra sheep, nor forgetting either that as these disappear down carnivore gullets at the rate of five per diem, their allotment of daily food will diminish steadily. Their total number averaged over the year is thus a mere 912, which simplifies provisioning. All the needed hay can be stowed on the second deck. A frenzy of calculating next ensues; and lo, there is room for everyone and everything, including the Noah family and "utensils," extra room even for any species we've lost track of. Snakes, frogs and toads can subsist in the "Drein or Sink of the *Ark*," while rats, mice, moles and insects, who can surely scavenge for themselves, disappear from the calculation, like Newton's infinitesimals. The birds can ride on the third story with the Noahs, and Scripture is vindicated, and so is the Universal System from which a Philosophical Language is being derived.

Philology has not often been treated to so fancy a divagation, and expository prose would tackle nothing like it again until Beckett's Molloy evolved his system for transferring sixteen stones, methodically, one by one, between his pockets and his mouth. His object is to suck on no stone twice before he has sucked on all once, and several hundred words into his exposition he is bidding us watch carefully while he effects one of his intricate repositionings:

> Pausing, then, and concentrating, so as not to make a balls of it, I transfer to the right pocket of my greatcoat, in which there are no stones left, the five stones in the right pocket of my trousers, which I replace by the six stones in the left pocket of my greatcoat. At this stage then the left pocket of my greatcoat is again empty of stones, while the right pocket of my greatcoat is again supplied, and in the right way, that is to say with other stones than those I have just sucked. These other stones I then begin to suck, one after the other, and to transfer as I go along to the left pocket of my greatcoat, being absolutely certain, as far as one can be in an affair of this kind, that I am not sucking the same stones as a moment before, but others. And when the right pocket of my greatcoat is again empty (of stones) . . . [several hundred words more]

Such systems as that of Wilkins had a great vogue for half a century. Their impulse was to order and tidy what previously had been random human behavior: had been, in one word, babble. Like Molloy, Beckett's Clov has a passion for order too:

> I love order. It's my dream. A world where all would be silent and still, and each thing in its last place, under the last dust.

"Silent and still," that's an odd way for language to be; yet the artificial languages, since no one spoke them, were silent and still indeed. Within half a century they were heard of no more. Yet in 1852 Peter Mark Roget resurrected the Wilkins taxonomy as a finding-system for his *Thesaurus*. All those years the systematizing impulse had never disappeared. It was subsumed into the written conventions of actual languages like English and French, which in their unreformed state were but the noisy behavior of Englishmen and Frenchmen. What emerged in the seventeenth century was the cult of the well-formed sentence, disposing well-defined terms: in France, Cartesian prose, in English, Royal Society prose. The famous specifications for the latter—"a close, naked, natural way of Speaking; positive Expressions, clear Senses"—had been set forth in the *History of the Royal Society* by Thomas Sprat, disciple of John Wilkins himself. Their object was "to bring all things as near to the mathematicall Plainness" as was humanly possible. Reflecting on the juxtaposition of "naked" with "natural," we perceive that Sprat, like Wilkins, took Revelation seriously: what method might restore would approximate to the prelapsarian speech of naked Adam.*

2

At Trinity, Beckett wrote a Master's dissertation on Descartes. In France, two decades later, we find him composing Cartesian sentences like the following:

Not that Watt felt calm and free and glad, for he did not, and had never done so. But he thought that perhaps he

* See the Appendix.

91

felt calm and free and glad, or if not calm and free and glad, at least calm and free, or free and glad, or glad and calm, or if not calm and free, or free and glad, or glad and calm, at least calm, or free, or glad, without knowing it.

This is brought as close to the mathematical plainness as may be, since, as the careful reader will have noticed, every possible combination of calm and free and glad, by threes, by twos, or by ones, has been accounted for. Thus literally everything it is possible to say has been said. We have also a categorical statement that Watt had never felt any of these things, in any combination, and a second statement, that he thought he might have had one of the possible feelings without his knowledge. So you can think that you did not know that you had a feeling; yes, that is logically possible. Any thought at all that pertains to the unknown is logically possible, so long as it does not contradict the logic of thought, which need not coincide with the texture of human experience. We note, moreover, that this whole virtuoso exercise, all seventy-five words of it, contains but four words of more than a single syllable; these are *never, perhaps, without,* and *knowing.* We are close to the economy of algebra with its signs and brackets; we are close to a Calculus of Propositions:

$$[c + f + g] \textbf{ OR } [(c + f) \text{ or } (f + g) \text{ or } (g + c)] \textbf{ OR } [c \text{ or } f \text{ or } g]$$

And we're close to the languages of digital computers, which weren't heard of till a decade after *Watt* was written, though their logical rites, thanks to Dublin's Hamilton and England's Boole, were already a century old.

Beckett himself puts their principle nicely, when he has

Hamm reflect on the liabilities of keeping a perfectly docile servant: "Ah the creatures, the creatures, everything has to be explained to them." As it does. A program for a digital computer must define all its terms and represent them symbolically. It must also account for every possibility, else some day some rare unforeseen combination may slip through and cause a malfunction. Such a failure to foresee is called a bug, after a moth that flew into some relay contacts at Harvard in 1944, and gained immortality in its moment of immolation. It is preserved under Scotch Tape between pages of a logbook in a museum in Virginia, the way Homer is preserved by textuality. The calculations of Wilkins about sheep and the Ark, as that moth can remind us, helped debug a system.

What Beckett had perceived by 1944 is that a declarative sentence implies a map of possibilities, most of which it does not choose to specify. "John went to the store": that statement is incomplete since it does not specify what else John might have done, not omitting his option of doing nothing. *Watt* (written in 1944) aspires again and again to exhaustiveness of statement.

There are sentences in *Watt* that cry out for flowcharting, so orderly is their display of branching options.

> Mrs. Gorman called every Thursday, except when she was indisposed. Then she did not call, but stayed at home, in bed, or in a comfortable chair, before the fire if the weather was cold, and by the open window if the weather was warm, and, if the weather was neither cold nor warm, by the closed window or before the empty hearth.

Here all happenings are choices among options, in a field defined without ambiguity, and closed. We can even map

93

it in an approximation to the Pascal language of programming:

```
PROGRAM MrsGorman (Input, Output);
CONST
    Indifferent = 60;
VAR
    Thursday, Indisposed, Called : BOOLEAN;
    Bed, Chair, Hearth, Fire, Window, Open : BOOLEAN;
    Rand, Temperature : INTEGER;
BEGIN {Main program}
IF Thursday THEN
  IF NOT (Indisposed)
    THEN Called := True
  ELSE {If Indisposed}
    Called := False;
  IF NOT Called THEN Random;
        IF Rand = 0 THEN (Bed)
          ELSE {if Rand = 1 then}
          BEGIN {Else}
            IF Temperature < Indifferent
              THEN (Chair and Hearth AND Fire)
            ELSE IF Temperature > Indifferent
              THEN (Chair AND Window AND Open)
            ELSE IF Temperature = Indifferent THEN
              BEGIN {Else if}
                Random;
                IF Rand = 0
                  THEN (Chair and Window AND NOT Open)
                ELSE {if Rand = 1 then}
                  (Chair AND Hearth AND NOT Fire)
              END {Else if}
          END {Else}
END. {Main program}
```

Inspection of Beckett's sentence and of the program will disclose moments when Mrs. Gorman must decide according to criteria that aren't stated. For those moments I have supposed a Random function, which would give us, like a coin toss, "0" or "1." I've omitted its details. I've also skipped saying how the program learns the initial conditions: whether it's Thursday, what the weather is like, and whether Mrs. Gorman is indisposed. These are details. Otherwise it is reasonably idiomatic Pascal, though if you're fluent in that language you'll have noticed that it doesn't give the computer anything to do.

All it possibly could do is state whether, given certain initial conditions, certain outcomes were true or not. Mrs. Gorman

> came, yes/no
> didn't come, yes/no;

if she didn't come then she stayed home:

> in bed, yes/no
> in chair, yes/no;

if in chair, then

> by hearth, yes/no
> by window, yes/no;

if by hearth, then fire burning, yes/no;
if by window, then window open, yes/no.
Having ascertained these pivotal yesses and noes, the program, like the sentence, dies away a little feebly, since it tells us nothing about what happened when Mrs. Gorman came, or about her sensations when she did not come. Is

she snug, in her chair, by the fire? Elated, in her chair, by the open window? Does she wish she were not indisposed, and able to come to Watt? Does not being with Watt play some part in any longing not to be indisposed? Indeed, what is the nature of her visits to Watt, when they do occur? Reluctant? Dutiful? Joyful? Ecstatic? Indifferent? Glum?

We are not confronting the limitations of a machine, its incapacity for feeling (though we notice that if it felt, it might be, like Watt, uncertain if it was feeling). We are up against certain incapacities defined by Beckett's language. We followed him in relinquishing all questions of feeling once we'd defined terms like Bed, Chair, Window, Hearth as "Boolean," which is computerese for whatever has but two states, merely yes and no. That is a reductive way to handle words redolent of comfort, but Beckett's sentence gives us no authority to handle them in any other way. To say as much is to say that Beckett's sentence is already written in a proto-computer-language: its options, its branches, take precedence over its verbs and nouns.

"Bed" is an English word potent with feeling. So is "hearth." But these words occur in our sentence not as attractors of feeling but as items in a set of options: here "bed" is but the alternate to "chair," and "hearth" to "window." *All* meaning, so Saussurean linguistics will assure us, derives from sets of options; if "in bed" is one place you can be when you are at home, then in a chair is another, and on a sofa another, and walking to the telephone yet another. To say "in bed" is merely to exclude the other members of an unstated set. Saussurean linguistics got formulated in our century, by Ferdinand de Saussure (1857–1913). It's been a powerful force for seven decades. Whether Beckett at the time of *Watt* had heard of it is uncertain, but his antennae were attuned to like stirrings.

3

They are somehow skew; when I say "I am at home" I seem to be saying more than "I am at a certain address, though I might be at some other." "Home" is one of the most resonant of English words; your home is your own safe and sheltered place, your rooted abode, the place of your sacred things: what the Romans meant when they invoked the *lares et penates,* the gods of one's home and hearth. But note that such feelings can not survive a demand that we define our terms; note too that orderly syntax detracts from feeling, insisting as it does on what Swift, defining "style," called "proper words in proper places." We're aware, as we encounter "proper words," that they're not the improper words they might have been; so the mind drifts away from them to their surrogates. And for that very reason a display of orderly syntax, in celebrating the exactness of each word's placement, can drain off the potential of any word to evoke feeling. If verse does not drain off that potential, it is because verse foregrounds its rhythmic schemes instead of its syntax. When rhythmic scheme and syntax mapped one another, as in the eighteenth century couplet, then feeling was notably schematized, attenuated. There is something menacing about syntactic order, and that menace is at the heart of Beckett's best comic effects.

Syntactic structures are not especially numerous. Subject → Verb → Object is the chief of them, and at several points, by several devices, we can hang on it chains of qualification or deferral. The letters of the alphabet are not numerous either, compared with the repertory of human sounds, human inflections. Written language may be notable for its poverty of resource, and exceptional for what it can induce us to supply, under the illusion that we find it in the text. It can be amazing what is not in the text. Little Oliver asking for more is a scene Dickens barely bothered to write; when we remember it we're remembering someone's allusion which in turn remembers an illustration by Cruikshank.

Frequently Beckett is rewriting the conventions of fiction so we can see how little is in the texts we remember, those chronicles of love and passion, of pleasure and motive and nuance. How reducible they are to lists of stated and unstated possibilities! Lately Jacques Derrida has attracted immense notoriety by doing essentially that. When Beckett wrote *Watt* in 1944, he was busy deconstructing the English novel with Derrida a mere fourteen years old. He did so by obeying every writing-master's injunctions: to observe closely, to construct the sentences accurately. By such means he goes on to tell us what Mrs. Gorman did when she called on Watt. What she did was sit on Watt's knee. There were even occasional kisses.

> But Mrs. Gorman did not always sit on Watt, for sometimes Watt sat on Mrs. Gorman. Some days Mrs. Gorman was on Watt all the time, other days Watt was on Mrs. Gorman. Nor were there lacking days when Mrs. Gorman began by sitting on Watt, and ended by having Watt sitting on her, or when Watt began by sitting on Mrs. Gorman, and ended by having Mrs. Gorman sitting on him. For Watt was apt to tire, before the time came for Mrs.

Gorman to take her leave, of having Mrs. Gorman sitting on him, or of sitting himself on Mrs. Gorman. Then, if it was Mrs. Gorman on Watt, and not Watt on Mrs. Gorman, then he would urge her gently off his lap, to her feet, on the floor, and he himself rise, until they who but a moment before had both been seated, she on him, he on the chair, now stood, side by side, on their feet, on the floor. And then together they would sink to rest, Watt and Mrs. Gorman, the latter on the chair, the former on the latter. . . .

That omits nothing of what it undertakes to describe, and has not one affecting word in it. "Farewell to . . . love," as Krapp in another Beckett work wrote in his ledger. A Farewell to Love is the substance of such a passage. It is pure choreography, pure programming: nearly a set of instructions, for a pair of actors to execute, or a machine. I'll omit the Pascal translation, with its subroutines, and point out merely how, if not a machine, it is we ourselves who are being instructed, step by step, what to imagine. Though the sentences seem affirmative, the hidden mood is imperative.

For affirmation grows dubious in a world that insists on evidence. How do you *know* that what you're telling us is so? No, do not adduce your opinion. Opinion is not scientific, and the word "scientific" comes to mean "trust nobody." Hence the discipline of a scientific paper; you describe in detail what you did, and what happened, implying that anybody else can repeat the process. That resembles the scenario of a poem by Wordsworth. ("I wandered lonely as a cloud . . ." can tell us how to get started.) It is also possible to assert that sets are, or are not, or are partially, subsets of other sets, as anyone may verify by retracing the reasoning. We have implied that many paragraphs in Beckett's *Watt* use that strategy. You may not be sure at all about the facts the paragraph seems to be stating, but you can surely verify its utter coherence; translating into some programming language is one way to test that.

But another thing you can do is issue orders. In doing that you come even closer to the spirit of the programming languages, FORTRAN and Pascal and their many siblings, since they are unique in having but one mood, the imperative. Despite appearances, they permit no affirmamations. For into an affirmation the psyche flows. Having affirmed, I am committed. "It is a beautiful evening": I have said it. And as I say it a meaning attaches to "I," and to commitment, and to the words "beautiful" and "evening," which I underwrite, saying something is so, having seen that it is so. But a sour and meager withdrawal of the personality accompanies the issuance of trivial orders. *Endgame* again, with Hamm in his mobile chair:

> HAMM   Put me right in the center!
> CLOV   I'll go and get the tape.
> HAMM   Roughly! Roughly!
>   (*Clov moves the chair slightly.*)
>   Bang in the center!
> CLOV   There!
>   (*Pause.*)
> HAMM   I feel a little too far to the left.
>   (*Clov moves chair slightly.*)
>   Now I feel a little too far to the right.
>   (*Clov moves chair slightly.*)
>   I feel a little too far forward.
>   (*Clov moves chair slightly.*)
>   Now I feel a little too far back.

> (*Clov moves chair slightly.*)
> Don't stay there,
> (*i.e. behind the chair*).
> you give me the shivers.
> (*Clov returns to his place behind the chair.*)
> CLOV If I could kill him I'd die happy.
> (*Pause.*)

Happy, what a word. If *Endgame* is a play about the potential end of humanity, it seems to associate such an eventuality with tyrannic Hamm's assertion of utter control. But that is the lower end of a slippery slope at the upper end of which, back in the seventeenth century, we discern that novel fascination with order, and notably with the order syntax can exhibit, in a prose as well-behaved as any flunky. They invented languages then, and we invent languages now; the computer community has found uses for several thousand.

4

This is not to assert by rote that machines dehumanize, or that Beckett would underwrite any such assertion. For centuries, routines of trivial order-giving were preparing Western society for computerization: a list-comparing, paper-copying, bill-collecting society which had already turned vast numbers of people into machines when real machines began being invented to set them more or less free. James Joyce records words uttered in a legal office, eighty-some years ago; they came out of a head "like a large egg":

—Farrington? What is the meaning of this? Why have I always to complain of you? May I ask you why you haven't made a copy of that contract between Bodley and Kirwan? I told you it must be ready by four o'clock.

—"Counterparts"

Farrington was a human Xerox machine; nowadays the voice from the egg would scream for a Xerox repairman. And in advanced societies microcircuitry has supplanted Clov, with feedback loops to obviate Hamm's finickiness and center his chair. All rolls on wheels toward certain liberations.

Still, Beckett continues to revolve his fantasies of people who do what they must and cannot do otherwise. In *Endgame* they are not only the people the actors play, but the actors themselves. "What's keeping us here? What's keeping us here?" cries Clov, and Hamm answers, "The dialogue." After that we find Beckett loading his players (players!) with ever weightier chains. In *Happy Days* the actress who plays Winnie must spend the entire evening buried first to the waist and then to the neck, deprived of nearly every resource by which actresses ply their trade, reduced to as expressive a voice and as mobile a face as she can manage under the exceptional circumstances. The three players of *Play* are confined in huge jars; we see only their faces, as a spotlight interrogates them. Since the urns are to be one yard high, the directions suggest that they kneel throughout. "The sitting posture results in urns of unacceptable bulk and is not to be considered." And whoever is bold enough to play "Mouth" in *Not I* must be strapped into a harness to keep even her head from moving so much as an inch right or left, and be hooded so that we see only her red mouth, "faintly lit from close-up and below." She must carry the whole play and is never per-

102

mitted to utter a coherent sentence. Such evident constric-
tion and discomfort is a theme that can't be faked or simulated the way stage cries of agony are simulated. It's
unsurprising that these late plays are very short. Only
robots would be capable of three-act versions.

Or be capable of doing what the last stage-direction of
Play calls for: *Repeat play exactly.* Well-drilled players
will do their best, but a film would do better; unhappily,
a film would deprive us of something essential, human
presence. Though the humans must behave as much like
mechanisms as they possibly can, a mechanism would be
unacceptable. Ourselves present in the theatre, we must
know that we're in the presence of people.

They must respond to the stimulus of the light-beam
that turns their narratives on and off. They are evidently
in a hell where this goes on for ever (a long run). When
Play was first offered, a critic was heard to object that
Beckett had at last surrendered all contact with reality.
That was only a generation since the years when the Gestapo had led prisoners through their stories, over and over,
under lights. Critics soon forget, like people. It even seems
feasible to link the Gestapo itself to the iron disciplines of
orderly prose, which prescribe for you, sentence by sentence, what you are at liberty (liberty!) to say. Such prose
led to memos with numbered sections, and to minds un-
thinkingly minded to comply.

Yet no discipline, no saying. The only undisciplined
saying is the shriek. Even grunts bespeak semantic fore-
thought.

For Beckett's subject isn't politics, nor contemporary
history, of which any politics we may adduce is a tempo-
rary ravelled end. His subject is Man the Syntactic Ani-

mal, not simply the Naming Animal but the being who must order names into structure, for the sake of keeping affirmations elegant. How keep elegance clear of its asymptote, sterility? Beckett can do it in eight equilibrated words. "Happiness, too, yes, there was that too, unhappily": nothing more elegant seems conceivable, yet its bite on its own tail gives pain. As we wonder whether or not we shouldn't laugh, we may remember a sentence from *Endgame:* "Nothing is funnier than unhappiness."

Or a sentence from *Malone Dies.* Malone is diverting himself amid the labyrinths of creating a fictional character: another life, not his, at his free disposal! "And yet I write about myself with the same pencil and in the same exercise-book as about him." "It is no longer I," he goes on, "but another whose life is just beginning." Then, unforeseeably, in one of Beckett's great sentences, these two coalesce: he who is being born, I who am dying. The sentence is this:

> It is right that he too should have his little chronicle, his memories, his reason, and be able to recognize the good in the bad, the bad in the worst, and so grow gently old down all the unchanging days, and die one day like any other day, only shorter.

"Only shorter": a guillotine phrase. It has interrupted a phrase for the violins—"and so grow gently old down all the unchanging days"—and has interrupted it with the sudden logic that attends a switched point of view. Growing gently old, that is written at a narrator's sentimental remove. The last day, though, is "shorter" only for the defunct.

"Only shorter" takes you and me by surprise. Does it

take Malone by surprise? Seemingly not. There has already been something ruthless about "the bad in the worst," which is a logical extension of "the good in the bad" and seems to say that to make the best of anything is to be deluded. That makes growing gently old a cynical notion, and foresees the savage "only shorter." If so, then, the elegantly constructed sentence mirrors its constructor, who saw the end coming. If so, then the cynicism that seems to well from the very language wells only from Malone. And if so—it's the desperate "if" that Beckett permits us—then well-being, as in Mrs. Gorman's comfortable chair by the fire, may stem from the luck of an "if" and not be inscribed in the grooves of elegant syntax.

Epilogue

Technology alters our sense of what the mind does, what are its domains, how characterized and bounded. In 1976 the four-color theorem was proved, in a way that dizzied devotees of staid proof, who had not expected technology to be inextricable from a proving.

The man who posed the theorem was Augustus Ferdinand Moebius, he of the strip, and it amounts to the statement that on a map of any complexity, where any number of countries meet along common frontiers, four colors will suffice to keep them distinct.

The proof, a topologist's White Whale for more than a century, yielded to ingenuity abetted by an American midwestern computer, and it has this vaguely unsatisfactory feature, that in detail no human mind can grasp it. Euclid's beautiful proof that there is no largest prime number can be written out in full on a three-by-five card, but the proof of the four-color theorem entailed disposing of special cases so numerous and so tedious a tireless machine was all anyone could trust for the whole middle part.

Machine error we can discount, by running the program as many times as we please on as many different machines. The adequacy of the program we can check and recheck, as we can the reasoning that leads up to it and away from it. But gone are the days, the former spacious days, the days that stretched from Euclid to quite recently, when whatever it was needful to comprehend could be spread before the mind to be comprehended in a virtually instantaneous act of attention. Geometers used to speak of problems they could solve "by inspection." The diagram Euclid uses in his proof of the theorem of Pythagoras does not lend itself to insight by inspection, and much ingenuity has gone into finding one that does. A figure Augustus de Morgan drew in 1855 does make the theorem self-evident at a glance.

That had been the dream of Descartes, that the life of the mind could consist of irreversible irrefutable acts, things you could understand in a moment of insight. That was true, when it was true, only of mathematics, and it is no longer true of mathematics. We are back to confronting what Thomas Aquinas confronted, the need for a lifetime of study to half-comprehend a portion of what, unless we surrender reason, we must deem to be *so*.

Here and there a willingness to scrap reason is detectable. Do we but study our own methods of study, interpret systems of interpretation? Is all quest for sureness doomed to infinite regress?

Founded on faith in the possibility of insight—the Joycean epiphany, the Poundian image that can flash in an instant of time; on faith, too, that technology need not consign the arts to irrelevance, the Modernist enterprise evolved its verbal technologies, its poem- and novel-machines of intricate interacting discrete pieces. The technology on which it drew for tacit analogies is largely obsolescent now: as much so as, say, Dante's Earth-centered cosmos. The Dublin trams are long gone, and the linotype machine; the typewriter is going; Bloom's watch with hands will some day need a footnote. Already students need the explanation that when a telephone whirs and a man says "Twentyeight. No. Twenty. Double four, yes" [7.385] he has cranked the magneto and is now requesting a number. That world survives now, like Dante's world, in art. Its assumptions survive in the structures of its art: complex artifacts we even sometimes take apart for maintenance.

APPENDIX

Science, Axel, and Punning

1

Thomas Sprat, Bishop of Rochester in 1684, is a much-quoted author by virtue of just two sentences. I work at this page within arm's length of three different books in which these sentences are transcribed: Basil Willey's *Seventeenth Century Background*, Brooks and Wimsatt's *History of Literary Criticism*, and Barbara Shapiro's biography of John Wilkins, who sought to order the thinking of the learned world by devising a philosophical language for it to think in. Sprat was writing his *History of the Royal Society*, published under the auspices of the Society itself in 1667, and he was addressing

> one thing more, about which the Society has been most solicitous; and that is, the manner of their *Discourse;* which, unless they had been very watchful to keep in due Temper, the whole Spirit and Vigour of their *Design* had been soon eaten out, by the Luxury and Redundance of *Speech.*

It is instructive to listen to him warming himself up for what literary historians have long regarded as the classic statement of the principles of scientific writing. It is essential, he has already said, "to separate the knowledge of

Nature from the colours of Rhetorick, the devices of Fancy, or the delightful deceit of Fables": a cool statement of which he soon loses the cool when he confronts head-on the topic of human discourse. For his patience is overwhelmed by "the ill Effects of this Superfluity of Talking," so much so that

> when I consider the means of happy *Living*, and the causes of their Corruption, I can hardly forbear . . . concluding, that *Eloquence* ought to be banished out of all *civil Societies*, as a thing fatal to Peace and good Manners.

Man is distinguished from the brutes by speech, said Cicero, whom that sentence would have dismayed.

What dismays Thomas Sprat, though, is what an educational tradition stemming from Cicero has taught us to regard as the unfailing resource of language:

> Who can behold, without Indignation, how many Mists and Uncertainties, these specious *Tropes* and *Figures* have brought on our Knowledge? . . . For now I am warm'd with this just Anger, I cannot with-hold my self, from betraying the Shallowness of all these seeming Mysteries; upon which we *Writers*, and *Speakers*, look so big. And in few Words, I dare say, that of all the Studies of Men, nothing may be sooner obtain'd, than this vicious Abundance of *Phrase*, this Trick of *Metaphor*, this Volubility of *Tongue*, which makes so great a Noise in the World.

We cannot fail to observe how Sprat expends words against words, duplicating and tripling his nouns: Mists and Uncertainties, Tropes and Figures, Writers and Speakers, Abundance of Phrase, Trick of Metaphor, Volubility of Tongue. Only Eloquence, it seems, can contemn Eloquence, placing it among "those *general Mischiefs,* such as the *Dissention* of Christian Princes, the *Want of Practice* in Religion, and the like"; great universal evils. Only Eloquence, or else the practice of the Royal Society itself—a new priesthood, we are to believe, or a band of saints. And Sprat's voice drops as he utters his famous two sentences:

> They have therefore been more rigorous in putting in Execution the only Remedy, that can be found for this *Extravagance;* and that has been a constant Resolution, to reject all the Amplifications, Digressions, and Swellings of Style; to return back to the primitive Purity and Shortness, when Men deliver'd so many *Things,* almost in an equal Number of *Words.* They have exacted from all their Members, a close, naked, natural way of Speaking; positive Expressions, clear Senses; a native Easiness; bringing all Things as near the mathematicall Plainness as they can; and preferring the Language of Artizans, Countrymen, and Merchants, before that of Wits, or Scholars.

There it is; and the printer of the fourth edition, from which I have copied, emphasizes the point by embellishing with capital initials none of the verbs but all of the nouns. The word worthy of signalization is the Word that denominates a Thing. That, it seems, is "primitive Purity and Shortness."

But the primitive Purity and Shortness is the purity and shortness of Eden, as we may guess when Sprat conjoins the adjectives *close, naked, natural.* Naked was Natural before the Fall; after that came fig leaves and more extravagant clothing. And language, now, is clothing, distinguished by Amplifications and Swellings, not to mention Digressions such as the Necktie. Adam spoke to Eve with a naked Easiness, using positive Expressions and clear Senses, in the "primitive Purity and Shortness." He did not tell her she was like a red, red rose; not even Hugh Hefner is certain what he told her. Certainly he did not tell her that her eyes were nothing like the sun, nor mention the fire that stirs about her, when she stirs. "Me Adam, you Eve" mentions so many *Things,* almost in an equal Number of *Words,* and is surely not the language of Wits, or Scholars.

"The Language of Artizans, Countrymen, and Merchants," says Sprat, naming three classes supposed to be expert with *things.* "So many *Things,* almost in an equal Number of *Words*": we pick up the mercantile metaphor of equivalence, a penny a line, a dollar an hour, a word a thing. Things are real and discrete, words are their labels, and our ideal is one-to-one correspondence. Each thing has a name; every cat that wanders through the English-speaking world has the label *cat* spray-painted on its side; we can thus *say* every thing, though it is difficult to imagine what we can say *about* anything. Swift, his mind doubtless on this very passage, arranged that certain philosophers in Lagado should save words, hence breath, hence attrition of the lungs, by carrying about with them in large sacks the things whereon they proposed to discourse; they would open the sacks and simply hold things up. One cannot say what they were saying. What do *things* say?

In Sprat's discourse we discern the unmistakable accents of the religious reformer. It is not irrelevant that he would one day be Bishop of Rochester, or that John Wilkins, his mentor during the writing of the *History*, would be Bishop of Chester within a year of the *History*'s publication. The connection of nakedness with naturalness, the adduction of "native Easiness," the rhetoric of return "to the primitive Purity and Shortness"—these are the mannerisms of a mind for which the substance of history is the degeneration of pure religion with time, and the essence of urgent reform is the restoration of its first condition. It is nothing less than the lost tongue of Adam that the new priesthood of the Royal Society will restore. And the lost tongue of Adam was busy, we are to believe, not in affirming at all but simply in naming, since to the unfallen mind of Adam things were present in their transparent essences and named accordingly, and on their names being spoken declared themselves wholly, leaving no void to be filled by webs of mere talk.

A stronger claim for the mere reform of prose style has not often been made: a primitive Purity and Shortness will restore, once we have its trick, the light of Eden that played upon all things before the Serpent, prototype of Wits and Scholars, blinded our parents with his flattery and the Angel intervened with a flaming sword.

What ensued, alas, was nothing more edifying than Robert Hooke's report on the Dissection of a Dog, and (brave new world!) proposals for "several new kinds of *Pendulum Watches* for the Pocket, wherein the motion is regulated, by Springs, or Weights, or Loadstones, or Flies moving very exactly regular." Those are unfallen flies.

2

What also ensued, though, was a linguistic norm. The language of science is a language abashed, purged of "this

119

vicious Abundance of *Phrase,* this Trick of *Metaphor,* this Volubility of *Tongue";* for "the tongue is an unruly evil, full of poison," as the apostle wrote (James 3:8). It is also a language to be read with diminishing pleasure.

"Bringing all Things as near the mathematicall Plainness as they can," they came, did the priesthood, eventually to discourse in mathematics exclusively: in a language no one speaks, not even its adepts; and when Wordsworth evoked the antechapel

> where the statue stood
> Of Newton with his prism and silent face,
> The marble index of a mind forever
> Voyaging through strange seas of thought, alone

he told us that the presence of Newton the sage would be indistinguishable from the presence of Newton's unspeaking statue: for the sage is thinking in equations, and is wordless, and alone. There has been no such former sage, not Pythagoras, nor Socrates, nor Confucius, nor Jesus: these were sage in the company of disciples, who remembered what they said and preserved their sayings. Who remembers anything that Newton said? When he spoke, he was apt to be quarreling about priority of discovery. In his role of sage, he did not *say.* Very good middlemen such as Henry Pemberton, who published *A View of Sir Isaac Newton's Philosophy* in 1728, the year after Newton died, conveyed Newton's thought to those who merely read English:

> Fix upon any plane two pins, as at A and B in Fig. 91. To these tie a string ACB of any length. Then apply a pin D to the string, as to hold it strained; and in that

manner carrying this pin about, the point of it will describe an ellipsis.

He is telling you something to do. You are not to take his or Newton's word for anything; you are to repeat the experiment. For this is the new thing the scientist has to say: I have done something you can repeat, some new thing you have never imagined being done. I have (for instance) dissected a dog *in articulo mortis,* and by inserting a bellows into its trachea have kept its heart beating even after the dissection away of the pericardium; and such is the regularity of nature that you, moreover, may do the same. Pemberton's instructions for drawing an ellipse are not otherwise oriented: here is a curiosity, moreover one of planetary significance, which you may reproduce with pins and string.

And in Pemberton we hear a voice like the novelist's, a voice that was commencing to lift itself up in those years. Pemberton's book is 1728, *Robinson Crusoe* was 1719, and *Gulliver's Travels* 1726. A novel enables you to repeat the experiment. You can relive, plank by plank and crop by crop, Crusoe's recreation of a habitable world (demi-Eden), or Gulliver's disastrous encounter with the talking horses who seem to be inhabiting the Republic of Plato and persuade him that he would be better delivered from a world that offers both lawyers and dancing-masters.

As befits opportunities to repeat some experiment, novels were written in Royal Society Prose, low-keyed, unmetaphoric, crammed with nouns. They bespeak, in their dense factuality, a new thing to do with prose, a prose disencumbered of "all the Amplifications, Digressions, and Swellings of Style." Within a century writers were discovering a corresponding new thing to do with verse. No longer a witty piece of persuasion like "To His Coy Mistress," a poem was becoming an account of an experience—an experiment, by definition not repeatable because I am I, not you, and even I do not step twice in the same stream; an experience by analogy moving, even usefully moving to you, through the medium of my stark and rhythmic account. I wandered lonely as a cloud (if I choose I may insert a footnote specifying date and place), and how the sight of the daffodils moved me I trust my verse conveys, and how it is that oft when on my couch I lie they have power to move me again. So I have shared my epiphany. Treasure you up therefore epiphanies of your own, against the vacant and pensive moods that will come upon you. (And that, by the way, is an experiment you cannot help repeating, if you live: you will find that vacancy will come.)

Consequently there are unsurprising resemblances between Wordsworth's 1802 *Preface to Lyrical Ballads* and Sprat's 1667 *History of the Royal Society*. These extend into details of wording that seem not to have been noticed. Wordsworth's second sentence contains the noun *experiment*, a word he had already employed when the book was first published in 1798. These poems, he said then, were published as "experiments," to ascertain "how far the language of conversation in the lower and middle classes of society is adapted to the purpose of poetic pleasure." He had preferred, that is to say, "the Language of Artizans, Countrymen, and Merchants, before that of Wits, or Scholars," though 130 years after Sprat he found linguistic degeneration so far advanced that merchants afforded no model, only country artisans.

In the fourth paragraph of the 1802 *Preface,* Wordsworth reports how the "experiment" was regarded by "certain of my friends." Its object, as he now more exactly rephrases it, was

> to ascertain, how far, by fitting to metrical arrangement a selection of the real language of men in a state of vivid sensation, that sort of pleasure and that quantity of pleasure may be imparted, which a poet may rationally endeavour to impart.

(In passing, we may note the word *quantity* and wonder, how measured? *Quantity* is a word to use when you are proposing "an experiment.") And these friends of his believed that "if the views with which [the poems] were composed were indeed realized"—this can only mean if sufficient readers reported pleasure of the appropriate kind and quantity—"a class of poetry would be produced, well adapted to interest mankind permanently, and not unimportant in the multiplicity [quantity again!] and in the quality of its moral relations." They foresaw, these friends, the possible generation of a new poetic species, "and on this account they have advised me to prefix a systematic defence of the theory, upon which the poems were written." This is as gravely worded as a grant proposal in recombinant DNA.

And it is exactly that grave; for what Wordsworth proposes is a poetic mutation which, if it proves capable of survival, will affect the lives of mankind "permanently." (It has affected ours. And when he wrote the *Preface* Mary Shelley was lisping words; in 1818 she would publish *Frankenstein.*) It is a mutation to be accomplished by writing of "incidents or situations from common life" in "a selection of the language really used by men," and Wordsworth expects that as much may issue from this simple stratagem as ever Sprat hoped from the new priesthood of the Royal Society.

> This is truly to command the World [Thomas Sprat had written], to rank all the *Varieties,* and *Degrees,* of Things, so orderly one upon another, that standing on the Top of them, we may perfectly behold all that are below, and make them all serviceable to the Quiet, and Peace, and Plenty of Man's Life.

And the poet, says Wordsworth,

> considers man and nature as essentially adapted to each other, and the mind of man as naturally the mirror of the fairest and most interesting qualities of nature [so that] the remotest discoveries of the chemist, the botanist, or mineralogist, will be as proper objects of the poet's art as any upon which it can be employed, if the time should ever come when these things shall be familiar to us.

The chemist, the botanist, or mineralogist are no longer foreign to readers of poetry, whom T. S. Eliot has instructed in catalysis, or Marianne Moore in the culture of *Camellia Sabina*—

> Dry
> the windows with a cloth fastened to a staff.
> In the camellia-house there must be
> no smoke from the stove, or dew on
> the windows, lest the plants ail.

They have heard Ezra Pound identify certain "rock-layers arc'd as with compass" on the west shore of Lago di Garda:

"This rock is magnesia." The science least foreign to Wordsworth had been invented between Sprat's time and his: psychology. He was one day to arrange his *Poetical Works* on a plan guided by the Leibniz of associationism, David Hartley; they fitted a prestigious system and might be read as case studies in the operations of minds.

Wordsworth devotes two long paragraphs of the *Preface* to explicating the poet's close kinship with the scientist, so close in fact that only two things need explaining: his emphasis on pleasure (but the scientist, he reminds us, would quit were it not for the pleasures of discovery) and his decision to pursue an essentially scientific course not in straightforward Royal Society prose but in meter. His surprising answer is that meter is a kind of anesthetic; when the substance of what is to be communicated is excessively passionate or contains an admixture of pain,

> the co-presence of something regular, something to which the mind has been accustomed in various moods and in a less excited state, cannot but have great efficacy in tempering and restraining the passion by an intertexture of ordinary feeling.

We need not believe this, but it was the language to which Wordsworth had recourse when he felt constrained to give explanations; and it is the language of a sober and intelligent Royal Society virtuoso, restrained by 130 years' accumulated experience from the headlong enthusiasm we often detect in Sprat, who expected the gates of Eden to reopen for traffic momentarily.

For it was, we must remember, as a disciplined hermetic priesthood that Thomas Sprat saw the Society. That prose of theirs, which furnished an idiom for *Lyrical Ballads,* was part of a discipline meant to unlock the closed Garden by returning "back to the primitive Purity and Shortness" before men imitated the serpent in talking to deceive. In Wordsworth's *Preface*—not, though, in his verse—the hieratic note is gone; the poet is "a man speaking to men," and not with the tongues of angels but with those of countrymen. But Wordsworth in this as in so much else is exceptional, and we shall soon find the poets too rejoining a priesthood: under, for instance, the auspices of Shelley, who defected from the great vision of the Royal Society in stigmatizing "the calculating faculty." "Reasoners and mechanists," he tells us, are being proposed as claimants to "the civic crown" long reserved for poets; but all that they have procured is that "the rich have become richer, and the poor have become poorer; and the vessel of the state is driven between the Scylla and Charybdis of anarchy and despotism." So much for "the cultivation of those sciences which have enlarged the limits of the empire of man over the external world"; Dr. Frankenstein learned what that came to. The *Defence of Poetry* ends with Shelley's claim that the true measurers of circumference and sounders of depths are poets, who "measure the circumference and sound the depths of human nature," who are "the hierophants of an unapprehended inspiration," are in fact "the unacknowledged legislators of the world."

3

So the religious claims that were made on behalf of nascent science in the seventeenth century were being made on behalf of a newly prophetic poetry in the nineteenth; and as scientific language—despite Sprat's professing that it was

the language of Artizans, Countrymen, and Merchants—
had withdrawn itself from public comprehension, so the
language of poetry was about to do likewise. In 1890 Villiers de L'Isle-Adam published *Axel,* "the disdainful rejec-
tion of life itself," according to Arthur Symons (*The Symbolist Movement in Literature,* 1899). This was the play
in which Edmund Wilson found the key to literary Modernism, in "a particular kind of eloquence," says Symons,
"which makes no attempt to imitate the speech of every
day, but which is a sort of ideal language in which beauty
is aimed at as exclusively as if it were written in verse."
For, Symons explains, the modern drama has limited itself
to "as much as possible the words which the average man
would use for the statement of his emotions and ideas."
But "it is evident that the average man can articulate only
a small enough part of what he obscurely feels or thinks,"
and it is evident therefore that the real language of men,
despite Sprat's protestations or Wordsworth's, has no
priestly potential whatsoever. Science, says *Axel,* "states
but does not explain: she is the oldest offspring of the
chimeras; all the chimeras, then, on the same terms as the
world (the oldest of them!) are *something more* than nothing!" Which is pretension, because Nothing is what is.
Symons translates the following interchange:

—Happily we have Science, which is a torch, dear mystic;
we will analyze your sun, if the planet does not burst into
pieces sooner than it has any right to!

—Science will not suffice. Sooner or later you will end by
coming to your knees.

—Before what?

—Before the darkness!

127

To read Arthur Symons's *The Symbolist Movement in Literature* is to see a priesthood assembling. The book is a curiously strict counterpart to Thomas Sprat's *History of the Royal Society,* by then 232 years in the past, in elucidating an exactly analogous movement, an effort to conscript the highest thought on behalf of men's liberation from common opinion, thereby coming closer (Symons said) "to everything in humanity that may have begun before the world and may outlast it."

"Here, then, in this revolt against exteriority, against rhetoric, against a materialistic tradition . . . literature, bowed down by so many burdens, may at last attain liberty, and its authentic speech." A revolt, we note, against, among other things, rhetoric: that "Luxury and Redundance of *Speech* Sprat had noted. And—here is the sacerdotal note—literature in attaining this liberty accepts a heavier burden, "for in speaking to us so intimately, so solemnly, as only religion had hitherto spoken to us, it becomes itself a kind of religion, with all the duties and responsibilities of the sacred ritual."

The responsibilities of the sacred ritual would have lain lightly upon a seventeenth-century English latitudinarian for whom things were things; words, words. The Symbolist movement was staffed almost wholly by lapsed Catholics, convinced in childhood that there existed verbal formulae of efficacy. Mallarmé rhymed the sestet of a sonnet on rare words ending in the cruciform *x,* having begun it with words to evoke purity, dedication, and the crucifiers' nails, contriving however that only the most pertinacious or perverse reader should be reminded of Christian iconography. These words will work what magic lies in their power unaided by associations of the parish. That sonnet ends, "Des scintillations sitôt le septuor," evoking at once the seven-starred Big Dipper and a countdown, *cinq, six, sept,* toward the mystic Seven, tally of the days of creation. Such concerns have seeped into all modern thought about poetry, and even the fiercely irreligious William Empson did not doubt that Ambiguity—a Symbolist invention—came in seven types.

It has been a cardinal tenet of our own age—Stanley Fish, for one, puts it forthrightly—that there exists no simple, no "natural" language. All language capable of any expressiveness at all reeks of artifice. Prose is not "natural" as compared with verse: Chaucer, who could render superbly in verse the naturalness of the Wife of Bath, was reduced to monkey chatter when he attempted a few plain prose pages of instruction to his "lyte Lowys" on an instrument no more arcane than a slide rule. In the *Treatise on the Astrolabe* we miss all those tacit devices of precedence and subordination that bring to the *Canterbury Tales* the tang and intelligibility of the real language of men. This is only to say that prose as well as verse requires inventing and reducing to rule and procedure, and English prose in the late fourteenth century had barely begun to be invented. Prose resembles spontaneous speech only in being unmetered, but on the strength of that resemblance alone it has been identified with spontaneity: with the Real Language of Men, who are thought to speak prose.

Men do not, nor women. As the tape recorder assures us, they um and ah and not only leave sentences unfinished but also, midway in what prose would deem a sentence, may change their minds more than once about where it is going. Prose, intelligible prose, is as artificial as any verse.

This matters, because the assumption that Adam spoke

prose is religious, not experiential. The Royal Society, when it proposed as an ideal "so many *Things,* almost in an equal number of *Words,*" was remembering that Adam was a namer—by whatsoever name Adam called each creature, that was the name thereof—and supposed that this was equivalent to prose: to a formed language. Wordsworth made the equally arbitrary assumption that "hourly communication with the best objects from which the best part of language is originally derived" (note the anxiety behind that doubled *best*) would issue, among countrymen, in a powerful prose to which the poet had only to superadd meter. And it was supposed by Villiers de l'Isle-Adam and by Mallarmé that prose is equivalent to the degenerate inability of Everyman to speak a tithe of what he obscurely thinks.

4

Prose is none of these: prose is high artifice. And when James Joyce proposed that Stephen Dedalus should be priest of the eternal imagination—once more that priestly image!—he proposed also that it should be the daily bread of common experience that the priest should transmute into the radiant body of life everlasting, by a means not always distinguishable from writing down the commonplace just as it was, but in well-formed prose.

Stephen was to complete the analogy with a priestly magician by taking vows of silence, exile, and cunning, the better, as it were, to enable James Joyce to write his first prose book, which is written (he said) in a style of "scrupulous meanness"—rejecting, that is, "all the Amplifications, Digressions, and Swellings of Style"—and much

130

concerned with words and the way people use them. In the first paragraph a boy is murmuring to himself the word *paralysis,* which sounds to him "like the name of some maleficent and sinful being." The real language of men is chameleonlike; words refuse to mean what they ought to, and a culture which does not observe this is a culture in decay. And James Joyce's last book, *Finnegans Wake,* declines to let its words anywhere specify what they mean at all. "O rocks," said Molly Bloom, "Tell us in plain words." But there are no plain words.

This is a grave matter. The belief that there were plain words sponsored the faith, three centuries ago, that science might unite mankind. After all this time of increasing disunion, in the course of which word-men and scientists have pulled so far apart as only to communicate through interpreters, we are coming to wonder if people only understand one another's words when they pretty nearly understand one another anyway. There are no plain speakers either, no plain readers, only groups of us more or less skilled in a greater or lesser number of overlapping languages. And this is not something that has gone wrong with our culture. What went wrong with our culture was the insidious belief that it could ever be any other way: that people could, for instance, just speak their "real language." That was a comforting but atavistic belief. It is only the people we call savages who have a simple, a purposive, a unified culture: whose poets are "technicians of the sacred." The decision to leave those simplicities behind, a decision we presumably do not propose to renegotiate, was entailed in our decision not to be savages.

Index

Air brake, 26
Alarm clock, 12, 20, 23, 25, 28, 34
Antheil, George, 41
Aquinas, Thomas, 110
Aristotle, 59
Augustine, St., 88
Ash-Wednesday (Eliot), 33
Axel (Villiers de L'Isle-Adam), 127

Baker, Russell, 69
Ballet mécanique (Antheil), 41
Balzac, Honoré de, 11
Beckett, Samuel, 15, 85–105
Bell, Alexander Graham, 53
Bible, the King James, 30
Bird, William, 49
Blake, William, 48
Blinds, roller, 20
Blodgett (tailor), 51–2
Bloom, Leopold, 11, 12, 13, 35, 73, 74, 75, 76, 111
Bloom, Molly, 13, 80, 81, 131
Boole, George, 92, 96
Brooks, Cleanth, 115
Brunel, I. K., 44
Budgen, Frank, 74
Burne-Jones, Edward, 47
Burnt Norton (Eliot), 24
Burroughs, William, 32
Buzz-saw, 49
Davy Byrne's, 75

Canello, Ugo, 57
Camellia Sabina (Moore), 124

Canterbury Tales, The (Chaucer), 129
Cantos, The (Pound), 11, 14, 49
Carman, Bliss, 15
Catullus, 28
Cavalcanti, Guido, 15, 57
Chaplin, Charlie, 7
Chaucer, 129
Cicero, 116
Cocktail Party, The (Eliot), 34
Colt, 7
Commuter, 20, 21, 34
Computer, 109
Confucius, 120
Cork, Richard, 25
"Counterparts" (Joyce), 102
Crippen, Arthur, 30
Crowds, 27–8, 34
Cruikshank, George, 98

Dante, 30, 80, 110, 111
David and Goliath, 88
David Copperfield (Dickens), 73
Dedalus, Stephen, 11, 130
Defence of Poetry, The (Shelley), 126
Derrida, Jacques, 98
Descartes, René, 91
Dickens, Charles, 29, 98
Dignam, Paddy, 75
Divina Commedia (Dante), 30
Donne, John, 19
Dowson, Ernest, 65
Doyle, Sir Arthur Conan, 29
Drill, 26

Dubliners (Joyce), 75, 76, 77, 80
Dutch shoe, 87
Dynamo, 12, 26, 63

Edison, Thomas A., 54
Electric light. *See* Incandescent bulb
Electric motor, 26
Eliot, Charlotte, 19
Eliot, T. S., 6, 9, 14, 15, 19–36, 43,
  124
Eliot, Vivien, 33
Empson, William, 129
Empiricus, Sextus, 85, 86
Endgame (Beckett), 85, 100, 101,
  102, 104
Epstein, Jacob, 26
Erigena, John Scotus, 51
*Essay Toward a Real Charac-
  ter* . . . (Wilkins), 86–7
"Etaoin Shrdlu," 5, 6, 8, 9
Euclid, 109, 110
Euripides, 46
"Eveline" (Joyce), 77

Faber & Faber, 23, 24
Fenollosa, Ernest, 57
Finnegans Wake (Joyce), 9, 72, 79,
  80, 131
Fish, Stanley, 129
Ford, Henry, 39
FORTRAN, 100
Four-color theorem, 109
Frankenstein (M. Shelley), 123, 126
Fry's chocolate, 13
Fuller, R. Buckminster, 27, 48, 49–
  50

Gabler, Hans Walter, 8, 13, 73, 74,
  80
Garnett, Edward, 72
Gestapo, the, 103
Geulincx, Arnold, 15
Giedion, Sigfried, 39
Gilbert, Stuart, 12
"Grace" (Joyce), 78
Greenfield Village, 40

Gulliver's Travels (Swift), 85, 121
Gutenberg, Johannes, 80

Hall, Clark, 55–7
Hamilton, William Rowan, 92
Happy Days (Beckett), 102
Hartley, David, 125
Harvard University, 22, 27, 93
Hefner, Hugh, 118
Heisenberg, Werner Karl, 13
Highgate School, 23
High-tension steel, 52
History of Literary Criticism
  (Brooks and Wimsatt), 115
History of the Royal Society (Sprat),
  91, 115, 122, 128
Holmes, Sherlock, 25, 29
Homer, 15, 93
Hooke, Robert, 119
Horace, 28
Horse collar, 52
Huckleberry Finn (Twain), 6

Idylls of the King (Tennyson), 44
Ibbotson, "Bib," 56
Imagist Manifesto, 42
Incandescent bulb, 9
Internal combustion engine, 9, 26,
  28
Irish Times, 64

James Joyce Quarterly, 81
James, Henry, 53–4
Jebb, Reginald, 57
Jesus, 120
Jet propulsion laboratory, 87
Joyce, James, 6, 8, 11–13, 15, 61–82,
  101, 110, 130, 131
Joyce, P. W., 65
Justinian's Digest, 81
Juvenal, 28

Kain, Richard M., 12
Karlgren, Bernhard, 57
Keats, John, 19

Kensington Science Museum, 40
Krapp's Last Tape (Beckett), 99

Laforgue, Jules, 19
Lavaud, R., 57
Lawrence, D. H., 6
Legge, James, 57
Leibniz, 125
Leonardo da Vinci, 52
Levy, Emil, 57
Lewis, Wyndham, 6, 41
Lift, electric, 25
Linotype, 5, 6, 7, 8, 9, 11, 14, 15, 49,
    110
Lloyd's Bank, 23
Lyrical Ballads (Wordsworth), 125

Macaulay, Thomas B., 77
Mallarmé, Stéphane, 70, 128, 130
Malone (Beckett), 88, 104
Mathews, 57
Mauberley, Hugh Selwyn, 44
Mergenthaler, Ottmar, 6, 8
Meter, 125
Metro. *See* Underground
Midas Muffler, 87
Milton, 19
Mint, 39, 40
Moebius, Augustus Ferdinand, 109
Molloy (Beckett), 88, 90
Moore, Marianne, 124
Pemberton, Henry, 120, 121
Morgan, Augustus de, 110
Morrison, 57
Moses, 88
Mulligan's, 75
Murray, Gilbert, 46

Newsreels, 9, 34
Newton, Sir Isaac, 89, 120, 121
New York Times, 69–70
Nijinski, Vaslav, 41
Noah, 88
Not I (Beckett), 102

Origen, 88
Outlines of Pyrrhonism, 86
Ovid, 28
Oxford English Dictionary, 64, 65

Pascal (language), 94–5, 99, 100
Pennell, J. and M., 25
Petronius, 19
Picasso, Pablo, 6, 9
Pisanello, 40
Play (Beckett), 102, 103
Poitiers, 51
*Portrait of the Artist as a Young
    Man* (Joyce), 10, 67–8, 72
Post-Modernism, 15
Pound, Ezra, 6, 15, 25, 32, 36, 39–
    59, 110, 124
Preface to *Lyrical Ballads* (Words-
    worth), 122, 123, 125, 126
Preludes (Eliot), 19, 21, 22
Propertius, Sextus, 28–9, 53–4
*Prufrock, The Love Song of J. Al-
    fred* (Eliot), 22, 32, 33
Prufrock and Other Observations
    (Eliot), 19
Pythagoras, 120

Radio. *See* Wireless
Railways, 55
Rathgar, 76
Rathmines, 76
Remington, 7
Return, The (Pound), 44–9, 53
Robinson Crusoe (Defoe), 121
Robinson, Fred, 55–6
Roget, Peter Mark, 91
"Ross, Martin," 66
Royal Society, 91, 117, 118, 121, 124,
    125, 126, 130

San Ku, 50–1
Sappho, 45, 47, 52
Saussure, Ferdinand de, 96
Schork, R. J., 81
Scotch House, 75
Seafarer, 55–6

Seventeenth Century Background (B. Willey), 115
Sewing machine, 42, 47
Shakespeare, 14
Shapiro, Barbara, 115
Shelley, Mary, 123
Shelley, Percy Bysshe, 19, 126
Socrates, 120
Somerville, E., 66
Spenser, 52
Spock, Mr., 86
Sprat, Thomas, 91, 115, 116, 117, 118, 122, 124, 125, 126, 127, 128
Steel pen, 55
Sterne, Laurence, 15
Stevens, Elsie K., 58
Stevens, Wallace, 58-9
Stevenson, Robert Louis, 66
Stoll, E. E., 79
Stravinski, Igor, 6
Streamlining, 42
Subway. *See* Underground
Sweeney Agonistes (Eliot), 30, 31, 34, 35
Sweet, Henry, 55-7
Swift, Johnathan, 85, 86, 97, 118
Swinburne, Algernon Charles, 51
Symbolist movement, 128, 129
Symbolist Movement in Literature (Symons), 127, 128
Symons, Arthur, 127, 128
Synge, John Millington, 15, 75

Tank, 26
Taxi, 25, 26
Telephone, 25, 34-6, 63
Tennyson, Alfred, 32
Thesaurus (Roget), 91
Tram, 26, 63, 110
Treatise on the Astrolabe (Chaucer), 129
Tube. *See* Underground

Twain, Mark, 6-7
Typewriter, 36, 48, 57, 111

Ulysses (Joyce), 8, 9, 10, 11-13, 26, 35, 64, 72, 73, 76, 85
Underground, 9, 14, 24, 25, 26, 27-8

Vergil, 28
View of Sir Isaac Newton's Philosophy (Pemberton), 120
Villiers de L'Isle-Adam, 127, 130
Vorticism, 43

Waste Land, The (Eliot), 9, 11, 14, 23, 29, 30, 33, 34, 35, 36, 43
Watch, 111
Watt (Beckett), 92, 93, 96, 97, 98, 100
Watts, George Frederic, 51
Webster, John, 19
Weinman, Adolph, 58
Whistler, James Abbott McNeil, 25
Wicker, Tom, 69
Wilkins, John, 86-91, 93, 115, 118
Willey, Basil, 115
Williams, William Carlos, 6
Wilson, Edmund, 127
Wimsatt, W. K., 115
Wireless, 9, 36
Women of Trachis (Pound), 57
Wordsworth, William, 19, 99, 120, 122, 123, 124, 125, 126, 127, 130
Wright brothers, 10

X-ray, 9

Yeats, William Butler, 15, 25, 48, 65-6